Diary of a Horsey Mum

Diary of a Horsey Mum

Linda Robins

ATHENA PRESS
LONDON

ISBN 978 1 84748 569 4

First published 2009 by
ATHENA PRESS
Queen's House, 2 Holly Road
Twickenham TW1 4EG
United Kingdom

Printed for Athena Press

About the Author

Ever since I knew what a horse was I wanted one. My childhood was spent running around pretending to be a horse and sitting on anything I could which resembled one! Even a cow!

My serious riding started when I was a teenager and I would ride any horse that had problems or bucked and I relished the challenge. All I wanted to do was become a riding instructor but when I was about fifteen I became allergic to horse hair, trees and hay, this meant I couldn't pursue my chosen career so I changed my direction to office work. I had a break from horses for a few years in my twenties and trained dogs instead and then happily took up horses again in my late twenties. My 'clerical career' has funded my obsession and love of horses.

Over the years I have had the pleasure to ride many horses and have been told that I have a special bond with them, I like to treat them as I expect to be treated myself. I think of myself as their herd leader and give them direction in their lives.

Both my son and daughter had ponies, my son still rides occasionally but isn't interested in owning one anymore. My daughter, who I mention in the book, is still the same and hasn't lost her love. My granddaughter, who I also mention, reminds me so much of myself when I was her age. So long may her love of horses continue.

My husband Allan, or my OH (Other Half) as he is known, has supported me since we have been together, well that is after his initial envy of my four-legged friends!

When I lived abroad I was extremely fortunate to have my own trainer called Jane, who was superb and taught me so much; my son was small and I used to wash cars once a week to pay for her. She taught me an incredible amount and said that I would devise my own individual way of training, which I have done. When training my horses I try and keep my methods as natural as possible and will change my ways to suit the individual horse. I don't profess to know everything, in fact I know I never will, but each day with horses is a learning curve and as such I strive to learn along with them.

I talk to my horses and tell them what is going on and never say anything bad in front of them in case they get upset. Some people find this odd but it is just one of my quirky ways. I also believe that horses pick you just like puppies do. Before you know it they have wormed their way into your heart – and your bank balance!

Linda Robins

Preface

Over the years I have been blessed to know lots of horses, some I have owned and retrained, some I have just ridden, but they all had different temperaments and funny little ways, just like people.

Allan, my husband, my other half (known as OH) always says that horses come first with me and humans second. He acknowledges the fact that he is at the bottom of my list of priorities and says that he only ever went up the list because the dog died. Well, he can look after himself, the horses can't.

When I actually thought about my use of time, it dawned on me that I spend an awful lot of it with the horses – but not riding. Apart from the mucking out, changing rugs, turning out, bringing in, feeding and washing feet – you just sort of, well, do bits and pieces and cope with the things that happen day-to-day. You learn to cope with little dramas and full-blown, serious episodes – such is the nature of horses!

OH asked me what I actually do all the time that I am in the stables, which set me thinking and that is why I decided to keep a diary of events just after I bought William. I have also included some very important lessons that I have learned while handling and bringing William on, as even though I have been around horses for, oh, years and years, with horses you are learning all the time. I have also included some non-horsey dramas which have impacted on my life during this time.

All of what I have written is true, but I have changed some people's names to protect the innocent! At most stables the saying is that people are 'either bitching or bonking'; I have written about neither, but hopefully no one will be disappointed, any bitching I have encountered isn't worthy of a mention in my diary and as such I refuse to include it.

I think that the first month or two with William were the most important and as such my records were written daily, then weekly and then at any significant happenings.

I would like to thank two of my friends Brian and Jayne, who after listening to my ramblings about the horses kept telling me to write a book, well here it is!

The Mob Before William

Our horsey family before William consisted of Ben, my 15.3 hh. dark bay thoroughbred gelding (fifteen years old) who survived a perforated colon and had a major operation, funnily enough not long after I got him. He was given to me because no one else wanted him, as he used to nap and rear and wouldn't go out of the yard. As he had a lovely temperament I thought I could do something with him. We found out to our cost that he was seriously ill, hence the napping and rearing episodes. He also has a dodgy back leg (caused by a thickening of the tendon), a patella that sometimes sticks, a huge scar round one of his front feet where his foot nearly got cut off with wire, is a bit of a drama queen and is fitted with the latest ABS technology brakes which give him a stop to be proud of. Apart from all of that he is fine and very loving. He makes my farrier laugh when he trots up as his action is, well, not the best, because his legs fling out from side to side. We do unaffiliated showjumping (SJ), cross country (XC), one-day events (ODEs) and dressage. He has actually been placed in dressage when there hasn't been a big entry! I love him to bits and we have been through a lot together.

We also had my daughter Ann's horse, Teddy (Doodies Pool). He is a 16.3 hh. ex-racehorse gelding (sixteen years old) and a beautiful bay colour. He has won money races and Ann got him after he stopped racing when he was seven. He used to flat race and when he ceased to be placed his owner tried racing him over the sticks to see if he'd go any better. He was last at that as well and so his owner decided to sell him. We went to see him, saw him walk up and down the yard, said, 'Yep, he'll do,' and took this long-legged, hairy monster home after paying £1,000. Well, there was no point in riding him as he didn't have a clue how to do circles or trot properly, he could just do 0–60 very quickly! He has a lovely nature and we call him Teddy or Teddy Edward and he and Ben are best mates. They remind us of the two old men in

The Muppet Show as they argue but fret if they are apart. We reckon they swap stories. Ann and Teddy compete in show-jumping, cross country and one-day events, dressage is not their favourite as Ann gets too nervous and they usually fall out, with her calling him all sorts of names and accusing him of not having a dad!

Last but not least there is my granddaughter's pony Midi. She is a black mare about 12 hh. and does everything but the dishes. She is an Exmoor pony and looks as if she should be 16.2 hh. as she takes a full-size head collar and bridle and is slightly chunky with little legs! When we bought her she was covered in lice and had to be clipped out fully, bathed and injected. Luckily one injection from the vet and a good bath sorted the pesky lice out. She is so good with Charlotte and lets her pick her feet out and fuss over her and drag her round the yard. She was Charlotte's fifth birthday present!

Living just outside a market town is great if you are horsey as you have the horse sales near you twice a month. My daughter, granddaughter and I just love wandering round, looking at the horses for sale and picking out our next perfect horse! There are some sad sights as well and I have to promise OH that I won't come home with a new horse each time I go.

You can also buy items of tack and clothing at auction. Bidding for tack is good fun and even if you don't want to buy anything just listening to the auctioneer, who is a great character, is worth the visit. Horses are also bought and sold and while I found it quite unsettling at first, I have learned that this is the way of life here. I know a few people who have bought and sold horses and tack at the market and it gave me food for thought for buying another horse in the future.

Ben was starting to make me feel a bit despondent as I seemed to be putting a huge effort into training him but not getting consistent results. I knew he physically would never be able to jump high and he had problems stretching over jumps and that is fine… until you have to do a spread or an oxer! I was seriously thinking about taking up knitting! But then OH said, 'Why don't you buy another horse?' I only had £1,000 saved, so something ready-made was out of the question and since I had previously brought on a three-year-old and have retrained a few other horses I thought *Well, why not go to the horse market?*

Ben looking thoughtful.

The Search

So… on the next few market days we went and looked. At least now I knew I had good taste – all the horses I chose went for way over what I could afford! However, our wait was rewarded when on Saturday, 15 July I spotted a little grey-and-white gelding. His details said he was two and a half years old, was about 13.2 hh., had seen the farrier and that he was to make between 14 hh. and 15 hh. He was tied up and was stuck to the side of the rail in one of the pens. He looked resigned to his fate but not horrified.

Ann went in to have a look at him and felt him all over; he was very shy and didn't know how to pick up his feet or to feed out of your hand. We reckoned yes, he had seen the farrier – especially when the farrier popped his head round the corner! We laughed when we saw the lot number on his rump, 1066, which just happened to be a number we picked for one of our locks at the yard! *It could be a sign*, I thought, as I had asked my guardian angel to help find me a lovely cheap horse! He looked so cute with his baby face and innocent eyes.

When the selling started we joined the crowd and slowly managed to get a seat right at the front. 'Tello,' as he was called, came into the ring and the bidding started, I held fast and Ann kept nudging me and asking if I was going to bid. At 500 I cut in, nerve-racking or what? The bidding ended at 600 (actually 600 guineas which is £630) and I realised I had just bought a horse – argh! My hands wouldn't stop shaking as I filled out the buyer's card, all sorts of things were going through my mind, what if he wouldn't load? What if something was wrong with him? After all, we hadn't seen him move, what if?

I duly paid for him in the office with my good old Switch card. When you buy a horse from the market you pay for them and then they give you the passport and a rope head collar to take them home with. Sellers are not allowed to sell the horses with tack or head collars. When I got Tello's passport it said he was a piebald and I thought, *But he is grey and white!* Apparently though, if a horse is brown and white it is a skewbald but any other combination of a colour and white is a piebald. You never stop learning with horses!

We rushed to get the trailer. Bless him, he loaded no problem, but threw a bit of a paddy and bucked and kicked when he was shut in. But after a few minutes he did stop and ate the customary hay net provided for his comfort. When we got him home and dropped the ramp he just stood there, he hadn't a clue how to go backwards. With a lot of pushing and encouragement he slowly backed out of the trailer and just stared around.

We had parked in the yard at the front of the house so had to negotiate past the washing line and down the step to get past the house. But Tello was fine and followed me, he just looked at the yard as we walked through it to take him to the field to let him go out with the others. He had a bit of a run round with them and Ben of course tried to bite him and wouldn't let him near his mate Teddy! Luckily I decided to leave his head collar on, which is just as well as he didn't want to be caught when I went to fetch him in to show OH.

After running up and down a few times I cornered him, made a fuss over him, let his new dad see him and then let him go back into the little paddock which is fenced off with electric fencing. As I approached him again he touched the fence, got zapped and promptly jumped over it into the bigger paddock. 'He can jump then,' was all OH said. That night we had to corner him again and Ann had to chase him in as he didn't want to be led, but he eventually seemed to settle in his new bed next door to Midi. He could still see the boys (Ben and Teddy) through the bars separating the stables and had a good view out onto the fields, so he seemed OK. He didn't know what a bucket of feed was and snorted a bit and backed off, but figured it out soon enough and tucked in.

That night, OH, my son Dave and I discussed the new horse's name as I wanted to change it. It had to be something to do with the Battle of Hastings as he was lot number 1066. OH said 'Hastings', I said 'William', Dave said 'Our William', OH said 'Just William' so after some deliberation I called him Just Our

William. His passport was duly sent off and that was that – now he is officially 'Just Our William'.

July

Sunday

Walked onto the yard with bated breath but 'William', as we now call him was fine in his new stable. I hadn't a clue if he had been in a stable or not so was worried that he might feel shut in. My thinking is that if this is going to be his way of life then he should start his routine as soon as possible. Our other horses have two feeds a day and so I started to feed William a small amount of mix for young horses and a little bit of Happy Hoof, mixed up with some water from the sugar beet. I also put in some seaweed and garlic powder as his coat is a bit dull.

After eating his breakfast I took him to the field again and let him go, I put a short piece of rope on the end of his head collar to help catch him. Ben still bullied him a bit but he seemed to be OK. He is still trying to kick me with his hind legs when I try and pick his feet out and he is also being pushy when handled and barging into me with his bum!

Monday

William let me catch him; I walked up and gently took the little piece of lead rope hanging on the end of the head collar and tried to give him some nuts. He made me laugh as he keeps his lips tightly shut and puts his nose in the air. This makes me think he hasn't been fed out of a hand before. I tied him up and Ann tried to pick out his back feet – all tooled up with her back protector, hat and sensible shoes on! She is getting quite good at dodging cow kicks! Bless, I think she is worried for my safety and that is why she is volunteering to do it!

Tuesday

William came to call! I rattled a feed scoop and all four of them came whizzing including William. Bless you boys and Midi you must have had a word with him as I asked. I had a think about how to cope with the cow kicking he does when you try and touch his back legs and came up with a plan – I tied a body brush to a short broom handle. This way you can touch him but don't have to back off when he kicks out.

Wednesday

Put them all out at 6 a.m. as it was incredibly hot. Ann brought them in about 9 a.m., Midi came first when Ann shouted and she had just put her in the stable when she turned round and there was William, standing outside his door waiting to go in. I put them all back out again late afternoon and when I shouted them in at night they all came, including William. I tied him up in his stable and ran the brush on the end of the broom handle down his back legs and he didn't try and kick, hurrah!

Friday

The plan worked so I persevered with the brush on the stick and by tonight the stick had become redundant and he accepted my arm on the end of the brush. We're getting there!

Saturday

We had a terrible storm and I rushed up to get the boys in. (Midi was already in as she is a bit too chunky and has to be on restricted grazing.) I shouted and shouted and none of them came; they were all huddled up against the bushes. I ended up running out in the rain and put a head collar on Ben to bring him in. Teddy was nearly hysterical because the wind had really picked up but he and William followed Ben in. When we got onto the yard they all tried to squeeze past me, there was water gushing down off the gutters, the wind was howling, it was dark and they were all hysterical! I shrieked at them and William, bless him, went into his stable, I put Ben into his and Teddy shook as he walked round the corner through a horrendous puddle into his stable. I was soaked through but made sure they were all fine and had hay before I squelched home to get changed. (I am going to get a hamster instead, honest!)

Sunday

Went to a show today Ben jumped out of his skin, won the working hunter and didn't touch a pole in the pairs. Showjumping, eh? And I thought I had the wrong horse. Reckon he is jealous of William.

Continuing the routine of tying William up, picking out his feet, same time, same place – yawn – as you do. You have got to watch his bum as his way out of things is to turn his bum towards you and shove you.

Wednesday

We had another storm midweek and Tony, who lives in the house, was so worried about the horses that he went out in the early hours of the morning and shut the top stable doors and put the lights on. I knew I liked this yard!

The farrier came to do Teddy's feet and gave William the once-over and picked up his feet. He is not sure William will make 15 hh., but we will see. If he doesn't make the height I want he will do for Charlotte as a second pony.

August

Ben and I went to a mini one-day event. His dressage was a bit hit-and-miss and Ann said that if he didn't do well jumping then we would bring William next time, but Ben jumped beautifully over a 2'6" generous showjumping course, including a big double and a treble with a scary wall, and had only one pole down. He went clear over the small cross-country course and we got fourth. He must be really worried!

William is getting better with his feet and picking them out is no longer an ordeal. I started to do work on the lunge at about a five-foot distance. Nearly got carted off once or twice but I just hung on! Am also getting him to follow me and when I stop and back up he does too, he is getting good at that.

Tuesday

Ann, Alison and I rode out into the big fields – which was just brilliant. I decided to leave William out in the field as another pony was out in the next field. Great idea, Linda! Anyway, we came back and the wind was getting up. Ben was starting to get hysterical because of the wind and then it started to rain. We all quickly whizzed back into the stables and I ran out to get William in. Big mistake – because guess who still had a jacket and riding hat on? William didn't recognise me with all those clothes on and promptly legged it. Would he be caught? No. He tried to kick me and I flung the head collar at him. Off he went with his tail in the air. I had to take my hat and coat off. Ann brought the other pony in as William wanted to stay with her and might follow. I promptly chased him round the field and wouldn't let him eat. A few choice words were said by me including, 'Look it is f***ing Mummy,' but I persevered. After about fifteen minutes he got fed up and settled at the gate and I made the decision just to let him go straight through the gate and into his stable on his own. He was shaking but I fussed and reassured him and no harm seems to have been done. Guess who wears his head collar in the field now? The next day he was fine and was caught OK with the others.

> *Lesson*: keep the head collar on in the field until you are really, really, really, really sure that your horse can be caught!

Charlotte is at her gran's and Ann, Alison and I all rode into the field again with William grazing. I think William looks to Midi as a mother figure. Usually she can't be bothered with him and chases him but when she is ridden in the field she allows him to follow her to his heart's content. I laugh and say that Alison is exercising two horses at once. He will eat a bit of grass then canter past us with his tail up saying, 'Look at me,' and then eat and do the same again. Babies are so funny. We reckon that when he is backed we'll get him to follow Midi and off he will go. I reckon his mum must have been black and that is why he likes Midi.

William is getting a bit cheeky at feed times. First you hear Ben and Midi shouting with their mature, deep voices and then William pipes up with his baby squeal. He kicks his water bucket because room service is a bit too slow. Not bad for somebody who didn't know what a bucket of feed was! I was looking at photos of him a few weeks ago and he has chunked out a bit and is starting to look good but still has a girly mane! William, you will be a stunner one day! Well, I am biased because I am his mum!

Been working hard on picking William's feet up and he is doing well. The farrier is coming on Sunday so I really do want him to behave! Went to the horse sales and bought a nice new pale and dark blue head collar for William. The one he is wearing is a bit too big and he could probably get it off if he thought about it. I bought a measuring stick and duly measured them all. Ben (the drama queen) was hysterical when he saw the measuring stick extended. William snorted a bit and backed into the corner; this seems to be his safety zone. Teddy didn't bat an eyelid and neither did Midi. Sometimes I wonder if my boys get the hysteria from their mother, ha ha! The end result is that Midi is 12 hh. Teddy is a whopping 16.3 hh., Ben 15.3 hh. and William (bless) is

13.25 hh. at the moment. Hopefully he will grow. Ann wrote it in the diary so that we can record any changes. He is getting a quarter of Happy Hoof and some mix especially for growing little people, so hopefully he will grow bigger and stronger. Told his dad (OH, ha ha!) that if he doesn't make the height I want then he can be a second pony for Charlotte. That went down like a lead balloon with a few swear words added in. But it's water off a duck's back and as OH says, I will just go and do it anyway. Isn't he a sweetie, bless, glad I married him!

Wednesday

A big day for William. As the farrier arrived, the sun was splitting the sky and he said to let William watch Ben being shod. I duly tied him up with a hay net and he was a good lad and stood and watched the smoke. Of course Ben was a little angel, hm! When it was William's turn I fed him carrots and he was pretty good, he snatched his feet once or twice but the farrier managed to trim them and they are looking pretty good. The farrier was pleased with him and so am I, the last thing you want your farrier to do on a scorching hot day is to have to wrestle with a stroppy young lad. The sweat was running off the farrier's forehead so I made him a coffee. William still doesn't really know how to feed out of your hand, he sort of bites at everything so my fingers were lucky to survive the farrier's visit.

Did a bit more groundwork with William and his smart little hooves and he seems to be getting the idea of walking away from me in straight lines and in small circles. He still likes to break into a trot and tries to pull me across the field sometimes. Had a think about the catching issue.

Lesson: when I go to the field I go up to William give him a titbit and walk away, this lulls him into a false sense of security and he doesn't know if I am going to bring him in or not!

Kept looking at William's mane and thinking that he looks a bit girly and so I got the scissors out and trimmed a bit and then a little bit more. It still didn't look right so took a bit more off. He seemed to like the sound of the snipping near his neck, so that was a plus. He looks very smart now – like a proper horse. I finished off with a brush all over and start touching his mouth and stroking his lips in anticipation of bitting him and putting a bridle on!

Teddy and William are firm friends now and groom in the field, Midi still pretends she doesn't like him and Ben, well, he is still the bossy big brother. Gave William a bit of apple, he made a face but ate it. Went to give him another bit but he just put his nose in the air. He obviously doesn't have a sweet tooth. I noticed that for some reason when William rolls he does it on the side of the hill with his head facing down… don't ask!

Ann brought them all in from the field. She gave William a bit of apple, he took it and then legged it! He is getting cheeky. She managed to catch him though, thank goodness, so he hasn't gone backwards. I did more groundwork with him, only 5–10 minutes at a time as his attention span is that of an agitated gnat. I rubbed him all over with the lunge rope, laid it across him and put it round him like a girth and got him to walk on. He accepted this and I am over the moon. I also got him to trot after me – with a bit of dragging! Progress is good and I am being careful not to rush him. Can't wait to back him in a few months time, so I had better watch my weight.

Did a bit of groundwork with William and managed eventually to get him to walk over a coloured pole. At first he snorted and backed off a bit and then jumped over it but then was really good and just followed me. While doing a bit of work on the lunge he tried to kick out at me…

Lesson: always wear a hard hat, gloves and back protector when handling a youngster.

He wanted to follow Midi and because I wouldn't let him he spat his dummy out! Will definitely put on the PPE next time! Got him to do a bit of trotting with me and he was quite good. He is good when left in the stable on his own when the others are working. He shouts a bit but can usually see one of them in the field so he doesn't go OTT. His stable is a big plus and I'm glad that he is in that one, it is right at the end and has a beautiful view. Something to think about when buying a youngster is where the stable is; the position of ours has certainly been a plus, with the see-through element and the view from the door.

Led William out for his walk round the tree. If I don't work him I just go for a walk into the field, down the hill, past the tree and then back in again. Got him to trot with me again. I also got him to follow me over one of our big logs, he snorted a bit, sidestepped and then just walked over it, very smooth, eh?

William is trotting nicely beside me for a bit longer and following me over some poles, which is great.

It is funny when you shout them all in and rattle the feed bowl; they all sort of ignore you and then either Ben or Midi will start to trundle towards you and then they all come cantering. William was left out till last today and he threw a paddy! He turned round, galloped back to the back field with his tail stuck up in the air, then turned round and galloped back to the gate. He let me catch him OK, he just had a face on because he was left till last! Looked at him and his grey patches are starting to shine, hopefully he will be gleaming soon.

Sunday Morning

It was raining and William put his head over the door and snorted and pulled it back in. I don't think he likes the rain. He also snorted at the water on the concrete but walked over it.

Monday Morning

I had my usual, 'oh no, it is Monday' feeling, went through the routine of putting the head collar on, taking the horse to the field then taking the head collar off. Took Midi no probs, took William – head collar on, head collar off and thought *oops*!

In any case he was fine to catch that night, Ann just put the rope round his neck – big sigh of relief.

He is getting better at letting me touch his ears and mouth. I put my finger in his mouth and got him to open it. He didn't even fuss this time when I brushed his head. Picking his feet out is still no problem but he does sometimes have wooden-leg syndrome – where he leans on it and just doesn't want to bend it up. I am sure he is playing with me, he is definitely not scared any more as he is licking and chewing.

Did a bit of groundwork with him and he trotted round quite happily on both reins a few times. Led him in hand and he was an angel, even at trot. I put my arm round his girth and patted and leaned on him and he seemed happy enough. Little steps all count towards the end result. Room service is still not quick enough at feed times for William, he squeals at me and then he tips his water because he is so hungry – bless!

Lesson: have a rubber bucket for the water – then there are no sharp edges to worry about.

On another note Charlotte had her first canter on Midi with Dad leading and running very fast. Her face was a picture and she looked so cute with her pigtails flying in the wind! The second time she fell off, but the third time, Mummy ran alongside as well and she was fine.

For some reason William always has to have a sniff at your face, if he is not sure of something he will look at it and sniff your face… haven't got a clue why. I suppose it must be for some sort of reassurance. If he meets someone new he sniffs their face! Maybe he was brought up with dogs, ha ha!

Ted and Ben went showjumping last night (we had a lesson) and when I put the boys out this morning William ran up to Ben and 'had a chat'. They were sniffing and then Ben told him to sod off. I reckon William was asking Ben where they were last night!

Julie, who taught us, seems to be on our wavelength. She had Teddy sussed when she said he thinks he is above us all and if he was human he would talk with a posh accent… that is Teddy to a tee! She said he looks as if he is fed up because he had to bring the baby (Ben) along, ha ha!

Because William is now happy being handled in his stable I have started tying him up in the yard when he is brought in. The idea is the same – pick out his feet, groom and handle him.

He is a bit restless with this at the moment and shifts his back end back and forth and tries to knock you out of the way. When Ann was sweeping he snorted and she was quite horrified, but I told her to keep going as he needs to get used to the brush.

Sunday

We had terrible rain this morning so I decided to let William go out naked – with no head collar on. I have been doing a lot of strimming in the field with a petrol strimmer. None of the horses bat an eyelid, even when you work near them. They like to eat where it has been newly strimmed, I presume this is because of the nice bits of grass under the nettles and thistles.

> *Lesson*: don't fuss about new or noisy things around horses – they will get used to it. The first time they might be fazed but then learn to ignore it.

I made William an extra-big bed as it is getting a bit colder and what a mess it was the next morning! His bed was just everywhere. He does what Teddy does – walks round the box. He is getting a bit tidier and pooing mostly in the same place, albeit on his bed. Now if I could only teach them all to poo on the concrete that would be brilliant. Hmm… have to think about that one!

Alex, who cuts our hay for us, phoned last night and asked if we could graze sheep for him. That will be great as when they have mowed all the lush grass down in the right-hand field, the horses can then go in that field. William came from Wales, it will be interesting to see if he knows what sheep are.

Ann thinks that William doesn't like her. I think it is just that he is so used to his mum doing everything for him. I think I will have to get as many people as possible to come and fuss and touch him.

> *Lesson*: if you are the only person to handle your baby then he will be suspicious of others. Get as many people as you can to come and touch him gently.

William nipped my bum today when I was picking out his feet. He then nipped me this evening. I said no to him and he hasn't done it since. He likes his titbits so I will have to be careful.

> *Lesson*: don't feed your horse too many titbits if you don't want yer bum bitten!

Did some more groundwork and asked Ann to lead him up for me. He was funny and just looked at her but eventually got the gist of things and off he went. I wanted to see him trot towards me but he is a bit funny about trotting towards people. He looks as if he moves with a nice straight action, but we will see, he sort of bent sideways because he was a bit scared of the jumps and coming towards me. We will practise that one. He was really frightened when both Ann and I went near him with our hard hats on. Ann reckons someone has tried to back him before, hence two people with hard hats on would frighten him… could be something in it! Ann also handled him and brushed his mane, etc.

When he was in his stable and we were all out in the field, I rode past on Ben and I thought William was going to come over the door. He was lifting his knees up and thinking about coming over. He stopped when I moved away though. Will have to keep my eye on that. If he perseveres I will put up an anti-weaving grill. I must also get a kick bar for the bottom of the door to make it a bit more secure.

I have been getting William to trot towards Ann and Alison. We stop in front of whoever it is and they fuss with his head and he is definitely not so shy any more. He is getting a lot better. He lunged over some poles on the ground – he walked up to them, stopped, looked and then just walked over them. He obviously figured it out for himself, which is great.

Ann got Midi's pink rug and put it on William, he was ever so good but pink is definitely not his colour. She then got out a noisy outdoor rug that rustles as it moves, now, that was a bit scary, but he was fine when she put it on him. She took it off and put it on the floor and that did make him snort but then he sniffed it and even walked past it and over its edge. We make a point of brushing the yard after we have picked out the horses' feet just so William can get used to that as well. Like everything he sees for the first time he snorts and then is OK. I have also started to tidy up his bed by sweeping the stable and picking up any poos while he is in it before I go home. He accepts that as well now. I think that as long as he doesn't have a bad experience with anything he will be fine – it is just a case of thinking ahead about what I want him to do and then implementing it in such a way that he gets used to it slowly. He now knows what move over means if you touch him gently at the same time.

We have got some cracking photos of the horses and have even managed to get some of the four of them with the three generations of us girls all standing together. Definitely a moment for posterity. I have a cracking picture of me hugging William, not so long ago I wondered if that would ever be possible.

Ann and I rode up the big mound that is in the field and the view is tremendous. Ben went up happily first, followed by a tentative Teddy and Ann. I forgot that Ann is frightened of heights. The mound is at the top of the hill in the field and it goes up quite high. Mind you, it was worth the climb as you can see for miles; we waved at Charlotte and Alison way below.

Ben and William have been grooming one another, hurrah! He is obviously accepted by his 'big brother' now. Poor Teddy, who had been grooming William, had to stand and wait his turn this morning, bless! Midi just does not groom anyone else!

When I brought William in and was taking him down the yard to tie him up he wanted to speak to Ben over Ben's stable door. As he did Ben grumped and went to bite him and William quickly turned his head to the side and whacked me on the nose. Ouch!

Lesson: never underestimate the situation and always keep your horse at arm's length if he is doing something new or talking to another horse.

William starting to fill out and grow up, although his bum is still higher than his withers.

September

Sunday

Have still got a headache and a bruised nose from yesterday's whack, but I rode Ben in the big back field. I just love it there. There are lots of little hills which you can whiz up and down. It is a great workout for the horses. I always smile when I am riding there. Ben is getting a bit strong so will have to sort that out as well.

When Alison went to get on Midi, William walked over and started to nuzzle at her back end as if he wanted to feed! Midi soon put a stop to that with a squeal and a sharp kick. I am sure he thinks she is Mum!

After riding I put Ben back out while Ann and I made some jumps, we made a XC table and another sloped jump, so we are well pleased. I brought William in while Alison was riding Midi. I suggested to her that she rode bareback so she took the saddle off and off she went. William was eating grass at the time so I quickly put the saddle on him and did up the girth. He just kept on eating and then when it twigged he looked round at the saddle at both his sides. He walked quite happily with it on – hurrah! Ann decided to try Teddy's bridle on him as well and apart from making faces when the bit was in his mouth he was absolutely fine. Ann said he might be one of those horses you can just get on and ride away – yeah, right! But all the same, William is now a proper horse and can get dressed, ha ha!

Charlotte stayed at home one night, so Ann, Alison and I rode into the big field and left William in the next field with the other pony there. Midi was a bit naughty so we all went back into William's field to finish off. Our friend was trying to get Midi to canter and William kept cantering up, bucking and showing off as if to say, 'I can do it!' His Teddy was right in the corner!

The next night I worked him in the field and Midi was in her stable, he was not pleased and the first thing he did on the lunge was try and cow kick me! I don't think so, young man. We had made a little jump for Midi out of logs and I lunged William over it. He just trotted up, looked quickly at it and over he went. What a good lad!

I've solved the knocking over the water problem at meal times. I moved the bucket! Well am I quick or what? I put it in the top corner where there are no shavings and he seems to be fine with that. If he does a poo at night before I go, I go in and sweep and make a big thing of tidying up just so he gets used to things.

Sunday

Ben and Teddy got seventh in the pairs at Somerby and qualified for Sudbury on 1 October at the BHS finals. We are BHS gold members and the competitions are one of the perks. Ben was absolutely pinging and jumped up the big steps beautifully. I told him to make sure he told William all about it.

Monday

I gave Ben the day off. I brought a synthetic saddle up to the stables that I had in the garage and put a nice soft girth on it. I also dug out an old bridle and put the soft rubber baby bit on it. I put the bridle on William and well, what a laugh. If he could have been sick he would have! His mouth kept opening and he was going, 'Ugh!' I left it on for a couple of minutes and then took it off. I then put the numnah on him and then the saddle and did the girth up. He moved about a bit but was fine. I took him out to the field and walked and trotted him and he was a star. He seems to have accepted the tack (apart from the yucky bit).

The mob were let into the fat field and Ann said that at coming-in time they were all standing at the gate bloated! Let them out but they were confined to small paddock – talk about disappointment! William couldn't figure out why he couldn't get through to the field. Put the bridle on him again (still looks as if he is going to be sick) and trotted him round and let him over one of Charlotte's home-made jumps. He is licking his salt lick and shoving it about the stable. I usually find it buried in his bed. Goodness knows what he is doing. They all went into the two fields for a couple of hours this morning. Midi whizzed off first then William, as usual, cantered. He was grazing at one side of the field and a big lorry passed on the road. Well that was it; tail was up and he galloped over to Midi. It was obviously a monster trying to get him! He and Ben seem to have a daily groom now, which is very reassuring. After the way Ben performed at the XC on Sunday (just pinged everything) I am sure he is worried that William is going to take his place.

Off to Glasgow tonight, mustn't forget to tell the boys or else Ben will have a face on.

Monday

Have been away for four days and wondered how William would cope without his mum. Ann said it was cold in the mornings and when she put him out he ran round and round to get warm, bless. He started kicking his water bucket over even when it was in the far corner (temper tantrum) but seems OK.

I lunged him with his bridle on. He still looked as if he was going to be sick but accepted it OK. He walked and trotted fine. I'm glad he hasn't gone backwards. He and Teddy were playing in the morning which was lovely to see. I am sure he will keep the boys young.

Went to get Ben in and poor Ted was standing there looking fed up. I gave him a kiss and a hug and he walked off. When I brought him in he seemed fine, however, when Ann came and checked him later, his back leg was swollen. He felt so sorry for himself and kept lifting the leg up. When Ann walked him he was dragging his back leg along. What a drama queen! She put a bandage on it and poulticed it.

Rode Ben while William was in the field. He started to show off and was following us, trotting and cantering. He whizzed up to us, bucking and showing off and then he stopped right in front of us. Ben just looked at him as if to say, 'Silly babies!' Mind you, Ben was good, he jumped over a 3 ft jump, wow! I think he must have been showing off to William.

William completely mugged his water bucket tonight so will have to move the bucket back to the front. At least that way he won't soak the whole of his bed. Will have to have another rethink. Poor Ted's leg has got swollen up all the way – the poultice hasn't done anything, so the vet is coming out. Typical – they are like kids, unwell at the weekends!

Oh no, am now the big fifty!

Monday

Brought all ours in from the field as well as the other pony, I thought it would do William good to be on his own for a while and that way he could learn to cope. He squealed a bit but kept eating and he was fine. I was riding Ben in the field and William wanted to join in, so he cantered behind us and bucked and farted and when Teddy came into the field he did the same. He did some lovely paces and stopped beautifully right in front of Teddy.

Teddy still has a bit of a swollen leg but is sound. The vet says the best thing for it is exercise. He has a one-day event on Sunday so fingers crossed he will be OK.

Ann helped me when I was jumping Ben and she whopped the jump up to three feet, argh! Bless him, he did it. The farrier came and looked at William's feet, William was ever so good and just snorted a bit at the smoke. William didn't need doing this time. The farrier said that his feet will have grooves in them while he is growing. He commented that he had filled out and was looking good. We've noticed that William, bless him, keeps eating while he is doing a wee, he doesn't stop like the big boys and splay his legs, he just does it!

Put Midi out, then William, and they started grooming! Hurrah! Can't believe it, she does love him after all! Well done, Mid. Haven't done a lot with William as I have been busy with Ben. Mind you, he has been exercising himself in the field when he follows us round.

I think I will have to dig out one of Teddy's toys for William to play with as he took his head collar down and had obviously been playing with it. The next night his hoof pick was on the floor, he is clearly getting a bit bored.

Saturday

The other pony from the field next door came back from loan was put out in the field this morning, which was of great interest to the boys. Midi just kept on eating. Ben and Teddy were prancing around and Ben was doing his usual rearing up and boxing and kicking out and generally showing off. He even managed to float for a few paces – did my jaw drop or what! Teddy, of course, floated round and William, bless him, tried to as well, the trouble is that nobody told him you have to hold your tail up and tuck your head in to look really impressive. He really loves to be one of the boys and made sure he was in with all the action this morning. I don't think he was really sure why he was doing it, but it obviously looked like fun to him. He seems to be spending a lot of time grooming Midi. I think she has realised that if she has an itch then someone else will scratch it for her.

Teddy touched the electric fence and got zapped and that set them all off again.

Ann let William walk out to the field on his own this morning, I said that is OK once or twice but I don't want him to learn bad habits like rushing, which is what might happen if he goes out on his own.

Did some XC practice and built a nice 2'9" by 3'3", solid-looking fence. Ben, bless him, just flew over it, what a star. I am still worried about next week though!

Teddy had a one-day event and I had a little word in his ear before he started. He did a beautiful dressage test although the ground was slippery and in SJ, although he wasn't concentrating because he could hear the XC, he got himself out of trouble and went clear. In the XC Ann was doing a really good pace and going clear and at one part she had to go round a jump. The ground was slippery and Teddy's legs just went out from under him. They both crashed to the ground. I watched Teddy get up but Ann still hadn't so I did a sprint of about sixty yards and just as I got there she got up. She said she was all right and I gave her a leg up and off she went and finished clear. She thought she had got up straight away but I think she was knocked out for about thirty seconds. I've told her to go and get checked.

On the way there some daft git reversed her trailer into Ann's truck and wrecked the front bottom bumper, argh! I *am* going to take up knitting.

October

Wednesday

I did some fast work in the left-hand field where the XC jumps are. William and Teddy came to the fence and looked. I think they were jealous that Ben was in there. I tried to tell them he wasn't eating but William kept going up and down the fence, looking to get in. He then started to paw at the fence so I had to come out. He cantered round the field with Ben and I, I think he was practising pairs.

Ann got bitten by a mouse. It was in her feed bin. I must have left the lid open a bit and it got in. Instead of shooing it out she tried to catch it and it bit her. She lifted it by the tail and let it go in the field.

Thursday

No one is allowed in the fat field because Ben and Ted have to do XC on Sunday, but they all stood and looked longingly at the gate.

Saturday

Ann fed them all and William kicked his water bucket over at feed time. She calmly let him wait while she filled up his bucket and swept the wet away, he was not amused!

Sunday

William's head collar was on the floor this morning and his bucket was at the back of the stable. Poor William hasn't had a lot of attention because I have been building Ben up for the XC finals at Eland Lodge EC. Midi has been babysitting a lot, bless! Came back after a really good day today, only forty penalty points over 2'9" course in the pairs – not bad for Mr Dodgy Legs! Teddy went clear, which was great. When we got back we put them straight to bed and shouted Midi and William in. He walked in on his own and I went in to pick his feet out. He went to kick me with his back leg and duly got a smack and an, 'Oi, don't kick yer mum!' Needless to say he stepped back and looked embarrassed and then was as good as gold. He kicked his water bucket over again on Sunday night so we swept up and did his water again and then fed him. Midi gets him going because of her hysterical whinnying.

Monday

Midi and William went out and started grooming and when I put Ben out he went over and chased them away – miz mog! Now he is a superstar he obviously is too important to watch them groom.

OH came up to have a look at the stables' roof and he wanted to see William work. He hasn't done anything for about a week but bless him, he was as good as gold. He still looked as if he was going to be sick with the bit in his mouth but did everything else well.

I've started to take William's water bucket out in the morning before I feed him, he seems to be getting the message about kicking the bucket and hasn't kicked it for a few nights.

Saturday

William and Midi cantered off to the fat field together. I put Ben and Ted out together and just as they were going out William started to walk back, shouting at them. They cantered together and William turned round with his tail in the air and legged it, he obviously didn't want to get mowed down. There was another pony on her own in the field next door as the other one had gone away for the day and William kept sniffing her over the fence and making her squeal. I don't think he knew what he was doing and Ben had to come and see what little bruv was up to.

Monday

Still not had a lot of time to work William, apart from the feet washing. One sheep got out, then some more got out, then they were all out! Every day there are one or two sheep out. OH repointed the roof of the stables with David and bless them, they brought Midi in because the flies were bothering her. She whizzes in when you shout for her. OH saw Teddy lying down in the field for the first time ever, we have never ever seen him lying down, he normally just eats constantly!

Wednesday Morning

Midi didn't want to go out and when she did she walked down to the bottom of the yard. Ben didn't want to come to my call and when I walked up to him William came running to get something to eat. He definitely associates me with food. Typical boy!

Was washing William's feet and he went to kick me so I smacked him with the brush. He did it again so I smacked him again. He seemed to accept that he had been naughty and was still quite happy to get his feet done.

Sheep have been jumping the fence, Ann and I saw one walk up and just ping it, I wonder if it would jump coloured poles?

Thursday Morning

Somehow Midi burst the electric fence and went through to the next field, followed by William. The ponies' owner's mum had put her two out and apparently some sheep jumped over into the field as well. Pandemonium ensued and with all of them running about the sheep jumped back out. When I got there the boys were in the fat field chomping and Midi and William were in the field with the two ponies, grazing. The sheep looked happy in their field. OH helped me to sort out the fence and I gave the boys a bit more lush grass to eat by moving the fence. Never a dull moment. Haven't been able to do much because of the persistent rain except chase the sheep back in!

Friday

Jumped Ben, who seems OK and then did some work with William. I am trying to teach him to stand side on to me when I tell him to stand and wait. When I was lungeing him he had a little canter on one rein and nearly carted me off. He is very clever though and learns quickly.

Saturday Morning

Guess what… three sheep out again, argh!

Monday

Does anyone else have a hectic life like me? My life since Tuesday evening has gone like this: got to the yard about 3.30 p.m. after work and noticed lots of sheep in the adjoining fields; looked in our field, no sheep. The other girl who shares the yard had thought the sheep had gone so had put one of her ponies in our field. After a bit of a discussion about said field, the costs of topping and a, 'Just because you have been here ten years doesn't give you the right,' sort of talk from me, ownership of field and stables was duly sorted and peace was once again resumed.

Because all seventy-three sheep were out and scattered, Ann and I used our ex-racers to round them up. With lots of yeehahs, some pretty nifty turns and with OH as gate monitor, said sheep were once again returned to their field. The horses had short exercise session as once again the fence had to be walked and then patched. The sheep had made a lovely motorway exit down the bottom so after lots of nettle stings, scratches and commando crawls under bushes the fence was repaired… or so we thought.

Went swimming with my son to get rid of some aggression. The next morning, I got up a bit earlier and went to the stables. As I got out of the car I could hear frantic meowing. I was fumbling about in the dark shouting, 'Here, puss puss,' when the owner came round the corner – nearly frightening me to death. Only having a puny little torch we couldn't quite see the distressed kitten. As our eyesight got better in the dark we could see it on the roof of a two-storey house, sitting on the chimney. The owner got two ladders and climbed up onto the flat roof, got another ladder onto the pitched roof and bless, the little kitten came down.

Put the mob out in the dark; the boys went into fat field (the field we are strip grazing which has lots of grass) while Midi (the fat pony) was in the other one. As it got light I noticed the boys were in the wrong bit of the field. One of them must have walked into the leccy fence (it wasn't on) and burst it, so they were having a lovely time. I ran over and started to sort it and Midi noticed what I was doing so legged it round and had to quickly improvise to keep her out. With the fence up, I went to get the boys. My two thought the fence was going to kill them and kept trying to drag me back from the opening and my daughter's horse legged it. Eventually got them all in the correct bit. Noticed a few sheep were out so legged it across the field and shooed them back in. On the way to the car, passed yard owner's dog, who had somehow got into the bin and pulled the rubbish out. Having a conscience I couldn't leave it so picked it up and put it back in the bin. And still managed to go home, put the washing out, shower, change and get to work with five minutes to spare!

Another unbelievable, hectic day! It went like this: went to the yard as usual at 3.30 p.m., and tacked the boys up ready for Ann and I to ride. She was late so went into the big field and rode and noticed one sheep was out. Chased it back in and noted the hole. Rode again and since Ann had to leave early to go to my grand-daughter's school I volunteered to rug up and feed off. Firstly went to sort the hole in the sheep's fence and just as I got there they all legged it past me and escaped. Just think how demoralising it is having seventy-three sheep barge past you into approximately 100 acres of grass fields and not being able to do anything to stop them. Quickly got out mobile phone to ask Ann to stay, but could I get through? No, so I left a message on her phone and ran back to the yard. Blood pressure at this point must have been through the roof. Phoned OH and shouted help, bless he said he'd be there in five. Went back to the stable and tacked up my horse, who thankfully wasn't fed. When he saw me with the saddle he legged it to the back of the stable. I pleaded with him to do this for Mummy. OH and Ann arrived to help. Put the other girl's two ponies into their stables (we had to go through their field). By now, the sheep had gone two fields away, so with OH standing guard halfway, I rounded up the sheep again. At one point they all stopped and stared and Ben nearly had a hissy fit because they looked strange. Some cows had wandered back up the field and I had to niftily herd the sheep through the cows but we managed it and off they went, back in. Chucked the sweaty horse in his stable, apologised to him, put the other girl's two ponies back out, let Ann go to school and went with OH to sort the fence out properly. The person who rents the other land came across on his quad bike and thankfully, because we know him from the pub we could have a chat and explained about the sheep. Went back to the horse and grovelled, apologised and thanked him for his help. Went home got changed to go to Pilates. OH was making a curry and didn't have any sauce since he had helped me, so I had to go to the shop and get some before whizzing out again. Got home and needed a glass of wine for medicinal purposes! Finally went to bed but couldn't stop worrying about the sheep. Thankfully they were still there this morning!

> *Lesson*: never ever have sheep, never argue with a menopausal woman and… playing cowboys is great fun!

William is turning into a hooligan. He checks to see if the leccy fence is on and then either shoves it or jumps over it. Teddy joined him as well; the grass is always greener on the other side. Alex (who was grazing his sheep with us) took his sheep away but left fifteen (today I counted sixteen, huh?) Anyway, they are in the fat field to eat it down a bit. William wanted to see what they were doing and kept chasing them for a sniff, but they kept legging it. They settled down eventually. Spent Friday night and Saturday afternoon fencing to hopefully keep the sheep in.

Put William and Midi in the near paddock while I brought Ted and Ben in and William pulled down the leccy fence between the girls and him and then went in there and whizzed round. The fence wasn't on, so don't know if he barged it or jumped it. He is a horror!

Took Ben and Ted showjumping, Ben got into the jump off in the 2'3" class, first time. Ted had one pole down in 2'6"–2'9". They both went really well. Midi is still getting bothered with the flies so when we came back she whizzed up to me and I brought her in. She really has a thing about them. Started to really chuck it down so brought the boys in about four, they were desperate to come in, William doesn't do rain either.

Monday

What a superstar William was, the farrier came and trimmed his feet and he was wonderful, I am so proud. When I put the horses out it's William and Midi who like to go and chase the sheep, they're so naughty. There was frost on the ground on Thursday morning and while Will and Mid ran off, Ben and Ted just looked at the frost with disgust.

The fifteen sheep escaped into the big field and after I had shooed them back in I rewired the leccy fence. Next morning they made a beeline for the escape route again and promptly got zapped. I have never seen such a disgusted look on anyone's face. They just stood in a line and stared at us.

William and the boys decided that it was playtime and they were all rearing and jumping about... except Midi, who ate! William was grabbing the top of Teddy's neck cover and pulling it and they were biting each other's legs. And William did a beautiful trot... wow definitely a superstar.

November

Had a lovely ride out on Ben and Ted who wanted to race in the big field, had a great laugh.

The boys all had a face on last night. Midi was near the gate and William came whizzing in. But Ted and Ben just stood there halfway down the field. I shouted and rattled feed and still they stood. I poo picked and shouted again, but they just stood gazing at the two ponies in the other field. I told them that there wasn't any grass in that field and to stop staring and if they wanted to stay out then so be it, as I wasn't coming to them. Charlotte rode Midi and still they just stood. Ben eventually gave in and came but Teddy no, he just stood. We fed off, brushed up, etc. and he still stood so I got a bucket and rattled it and hurrah, he graced us with his presence. Not sure what he was playing at but told William and Midi to tell them all about staying out in the dark with no good grass, so hopefully that will work. Don't you just love 'em?

Thursday

Shouted tonight and they all came whizzing. Midi was at the gate as usual and still scratching. She was whizzing round like a rocket as Ann had smacked her earlier because she wouldn't move. But she is a great little mover when she gets going. William was really minging again, argh, can he get filthy!

Seen the fox quite a few times, he or she is getting quite cheeky and tonight he sat and looked at us. Charlotte thought it was funny.

William is getting good at picking his feet out with me staying on the same side. He really is quite clever. He and Midi have taken to charging about the field, which is not like Midi at all and, boy, can she shift. Her little body stays still and her legs go ten to the dozen.

I have noticed that in the morning, when I switch William's

light on, he yawns and does a wee, he must obviously still be sleeping when I turn up.

The sheep have gone so Midi and William have nobody to grump at and boss about. Didn't go up to the stables one night but I had told them all. Well, next morning was there a face on or what. Nobody said good morning to me until I was actually about to feed them. Wonder what they will do when I am gone for two weeks!

Oh, we're going to Barbados!

December

Had a great holiday and wondered how the boys would be when I returned. Ben just looked at me and William, bless, was just fine. Ann had been letting him go to the field on his own, which worried me, but he is OK and still happy to be led and have his feet done, etc.

The bad news is that we have to find a new yard due to the big house being sold and a bit of a hoo-ha about the land. Been looking at yards and yards since coming back from holiday but can't seem to find anywhere suitable.

Ann thought she had found somewhere and we duly visited. She had talked to the owner and he seemed keen but then when we eventually met he said he had decided to act through an agent. He had someone with him (don't think it was his wife) and she looked horsey and very familiar. Anyway, the agent came back to Ann on Friday and said the rent would be £275 per month and then water and electric had to be added – er, I don't think so. There were only two proper stables and a sort of barn which had makeshift stables. We said we would modify them if need be. There was an outdoor manège and about two acres. The price should've reflected the current functional facilities, i.e. the two stables, but obviously doesn't. We would also have had to rent a field next to it for extra grazing, so that was a no.

Another yard was at Six Hills, a beautiful yard but at the moment there's not enough grass. The owner said we could have the field at the other side of the road but that is a no-no because I go myself in the mornings and I wouldn't be able to take the horses and keep an eye on Charlotte. I can't lead the horses and take Charlotte at the same time over a busy road. Still not decided about it though, we might have to wait.

Another one was on the other side of Melton, about five miles from me. It was very quiet with lots of grazing and storage. The stables were big but they weren't finished and they were very cold. Couldn't imagine us there and I didn't want to drive down the long, single-track road to it in the early morning.

We must have visited every yard in the area asking for DIY livery. Argh! Have had enough and have a stinking cold as well. Ben hasn't been ridden for three weeks and thinks he has retired. I don't think William will be backed till summer now.

Went to Long Clawson but that just didn't feel right. The yard had really high stable doors that Mid and William wouldn't be able to see over. Not much grazing and the fact that it was beside a busy road put us off.

Saw cracking stables near us but they only had one acre of grazing! Absolutely peed off about that as I would have moved there tomorrow.

Saw a nice yard outside Wymeswold but it was very isolated. The worry was that five minutes after you left it could be completely emptied – everything nicked, so that was also a no-no.

Went to another one about eight miles away but the owner wanted about £30 per week with hay and straw and for that price it was too far to travel… I just want to give up!

Meanwhile, William has lost a tooth, one at the top front. It was hanging loose and Ann pulled it out. He was very brave, bless, even though it bled a little bit.

Ben hasn't been ridden for four weeks now, so it came as a bit of a shock when I tacked him up at the weekend. He just looked at me in disgust. He was an absolute poppet though and no worse than usual with his spookiness. We even rode out the next day. What a superstar. William is a big boy and walking out to the field without a head collar on now. When they see us at night they all charge to the gate, wanting to be brought in. William is getting vocal as well and when he hears your voice will shout out. He is absolutely minging but I want to avoid brushing him so that he stays warm.

Mud everywhere, which is a pain! I cleaned a bit of mud away from the gate and a puddle formed. When I put William out the next morning he stopped and had a play in it. He was splashing around with his nose. Trust him!

January

The Dreaded Big Move!

Took three days to move, but they are all settled in now. We went for the one down the long, single-track lane at the other side of Melton. We are in a great big field down the lane at the moment and it is a pain because it takes ages to get there. Ted went in first, because of his foot and then I took the other three at once and they were fine. William is learning to lead on his other side now. He is being a spoilt brat when it is time to go out of his stable and he has become very fussy and won't eat the old hay. We have sixty bales left in the barn at the old yard but can't get to them because of the mud.

They are all on straw now and of course, what did they do but start eating it because it has nice green bits in it! Am a bit worried about a lack of poos because they are not eating the hay. It is very windy up there and Ben and Wills were being very spooky and a real pain when I brought them in one day, and I had to shout at them and whack Ben with the rope to get him to move. Wills was frightened of the rope but he is OK now. The next day he actually hugged me by putting his head in my arms. My first hug: 13 January 2007, a day to remember.

William seems to like puddles and quite happily walks through them on the way back from the field. He even stopped for a splash. He is being really good with his feet, letting them be washed when he is brought in. The weather was really bad and they all had to stay in so I left him with Teddy's food thingy. He finally figured out that you had to roll it to get the nuts out.

Ann, Charlotte and I rode out down the road and left Wills in his stable with his toy and he was really good. You could hear him kicking it as we were going out. He shouted when we got back but that was all.

Managed to bring all four in at once and put them all out together. Wills was biting Midi, Ben was squashing me and Teddy was behind. Midi started jogging so I had to shout at them, stop and then sort them out and they were fine. Just being lazy I suppose.

Their jabs are due tomorrow so while the vet here I need to get her to look at William's eye as well.

The vet came and said it looks like a sarcoid. He has one near his little man and one on the front of his chest. She said he could get injections for the others but the one near his eye is tricky.

We had snow and the road was icy, so decided to leave them all in just for one day, next day, well...

I had put William and Midi out in the field first, then got Ben and Teddy next. Was just putting Ben and Ted out and was turning them round to shut the gate (it is a boingy electric fence thing used for cows and is very stiff, it pings back if you let it go) and William had legged it through the small gap, closely followed by Midi. Took Ben and Ted away from the gate and shouted 'William', because he usually follows them – but I had no chance. Took Ben and Ted to the gate, shut it and let them go. They went off bucking and farting while Midi and William legged it into the field across the road, which is arable, seeded and about fifteen acres.

I ran across the field a bit so I could keep my eye on them while they did their lap of honour, which was not easy as the fields are still very wet and squelchy, and I did what any self-respecting horse owner does in times of complete and utter helplessness: screeched at them, calling them fu★★ing bar stewards. It didn't seem to help much but it did make me feel better. As they came galloping towards me they slowed down and stopped. William, bless, let me catch him and I put him in the field. But Midi – no chance. Off she went out of the field and down the road, showing off to the other three. Teddy was doing his beautiful trot and floating round the field, Ben was rearing and jumping and bucking and William was following, doing the same. Midi legged it back into the arable field another way and I chased her out back onto the road. She trotted up the road and slipped a few times, which slowed her down a bit. After running up and down after her a few times I sort of cornered her. I just got to her and she legged it – not to be put off, I did an impressive sprint beside her and flung my arms and the rope round her neck and dragged her to a stop. Hurrah! Score: Nanny 1–Midi 0. Put her in the field with the mob and off they went – whoopee – down the field.

> *Lesson*: never underestimate the intelligence of a curious youngster, and never mess with your Nan!

Now, that is not my ideal way of starting the day and made me run late. Since I have a seven-mile drive home now and have to go through Melton the journey does take some time. I always get stopped at the last lot of traffic lights and to save time in my tight schedule I decided this morning to do my Tai Chi facial exercises while waiting at the traffic lights. Not a pretty sight. There was me with my sweaty designer hairstyle, making all sorts of facial contortions while sitting at the traffic lights, so can I just apologise to anyone who might have seen me.

There are four dogs at the new yard, a collie called Tessa, two fern terrier cross springers called Tigger and T Spark and Annie the springer. They like to come to the field with us every morning when we go with the horses. The two little black ones always jump up and look as if they are dancing. Tessa takes either a stone or a golf ball with her (I have never known one dog to have so many golf balls) and she will stop, chuck whatever is in her mouth, lie down staring at whatever she has thrown and then wait for someone to kick or throw it back. If you don't oblige she sometimes waits at that point, watching the object till you are on your way back. If a car comes along she doesn't move, but keeps her beady eye on her prize. The two little ones run and ping up in the air and, boy, can they shift. They sniff and ping and whiz off into the woods. Annie has the waggiest tail in the whole world. She sets off sniffing with her little tail going ten to the dozen, then she has a poo, then she sniffs and then has another poo! They are all as mad as hatters.

February

Let William sniff some hot chocolate which made him make faces, bless. Midi liked it because she knows what chocolate is!

Let William have the run of his stable and the bit in-between, so I had to squeeze out through a small gap to get to the feed room. William followed! I think he has an obsession with gaps, as in if he sees one he just has to know what is on the other side. Hence the escaping the other day. I shoved a bale of straw through the gap and William, who also has to touch everything he sees with his hoof, pawed at the straw and got his leg stuck down the string. He didn't move, just stood there looking at his leg attached to the straw. I have to really think about anything that is in reach of his leg because he paws at it.

The sarcoid on William's eye was bleeding as he had knocked it on the bucket of water. I will have to speak to the vet and see what sort of options there are as it will be painful in the heat of the summer with all the flies.

William is getting very cheeky on the way to the field – pushing and trying to bite Midi and I. Will have to stop that. Midi has two front shoes on and is riding out with us, she has a permanent smile on her face.

When I do the water buckets and the hose is filling them up it always makes William want to wee. He walks about with his dingly-dangly hanging out! He is still fascinated by the big field that he and Midi went in and always heads for it when he is going out. Midi and Ben need a clip now they are working even though it is only February.

Took pictures of William's sarcoid above his eye and emailed them to the vet. She is going to send them to Liverpool University to have them looked at and to hopefully give us a course of action. She reckons it will cost about £800! Don't know where that money is going to come from. He keeps knocking it and it looks sore and ulcered.

Wills has to go in to the veterinary hospital on Wednesday to have his eye injected. He will need a steroid injection in case he has a reaction to the BCG that they have to give him. He also needs to be sedated and will have to stay there all day to recover.

He is really turning into Mr Nosey now and wants to explore every time we come into the yard. Midi has a rug on because she has just been clipped and he is always shoving her rug. I gave him the run of the stable and the bit in-between when we rode out and he pulled the offending rug down, he definitely wasn't impressed by it. He has spilled his water bucket over twice lately, I think it was because there was ice in it that he was trying to get rid of. We have had a bit of snow and he shoved it around and made a face. They were all kept in one day because of the snow and when Ann put them out the next day they all went loopy. Wills likes to join in, bucking and rearing and generally being stupid. I think being with the mob is helping him to mature – hopefully into a nice young man.

Wednesday, 14 February

It's Valentine's Day and had to take William to the veterinary hospital – four years to the day that I got Ben. He loaded tentatively, with wooden legs, but went in just the same. He travelled in the new trailer and stomped at the floor a lot of the way there. He snorted and squeezed himself into the stable and had a good look round. When they injected the sarcoid it popped out and there is a hole left. He will still need more jabs to make sure all of it has gone. We picked him up after 3 p.m. and he was desperate to get out of the stable and nearly pushed past me. He was a bit more wary loading on the way home but still stomped a bit so we knew he was there. I think he pawed at the ground like he does when he is in spoilt-brat mode. We let him out into the field and they all rushed up and had a whiz round with him. We were late getting them all in and when they heard us walking down the road they came cantering up. I think they thought we had forgotten about them. Nice to know you are wanted!

Wills was a bit lovey-dovey the next night. I think his eye must have felt better although he did nip the back of my leg on the way out, cheeky little beggar.

Took Midi and Wills to the field, they don't really like the mud so when we get to the gate Wills goes behind Midi so he can walk at the side of the field. Today however, he walked along the outside of the field, duh! Had to turn back and get him inside.

He was a pain going in the trailer on our next visit to the hospital. He threw a paddy and tried to kick the dog; he reared, jumped about. Sarah and Paul, who own the yard, helped me and he even pulled Paul about. I led him and he was half in and half out and Paul flipped the ramp up and hurrah, he was in. It took half an hour. He was a bit of a pain coming back but I told Ann not to bully him in and he wasn't too bad. Two more visits to go!

Moved them all to another field. Teddy has to stay in because of really wet feet so he has the run of his and Ben's stable. The other three came in really filthy. William was apparently splashing in the wet field and then had a really good roll. I have never seen anyone look so filthy. Have been putting cream on the sarcoid on his chest, but it still looks the same. When he goes into his stable at night the first thing he does is walk to the back and have a poo! Creatures of habit are men!

Took the big boys for a bit of a blast on the set-aside fields. Boy, did they whiz!

At the last vet's visit William shouted at Midi and he had his teenage broken voice! Bless! It wasn't so squeaky and sounded quite manly.

Charlotte has been to see the new lambs. She got to pick one up and hug it so she was really chuffed. She stroked a poorly one as well but we told her not to kiss that one.

William really doesn't like having his cream put on and pulls his leg up and pulls away. It must nip something awful, mind you, he is a man.

Teddy is being a right hooligan when out and is up on his toes. Not sure if it is the weather or because he is in all the time. Mind you, he did go out for an hour with the mob and they all came in really, really muddy – splattered all over with it, but looking very pleased with themselves. Wills and Teddy had a play and a run round. I think Ben finds the ground a bit too tiring.

The fence blew down in the field and William walked out, followed by Midi and Ben. They were all eating happily and then

William decided to go and visit the neighbouring horses and so whizzed across. They trundled onto the road so Sarah and Paul had to go and get them and put them into their stables. William wasn't sure about Sarah and Paul and didn't want to be caught at first, so they got Ben, then a reluctant Midi, then finally William came over and wanted to put his head collar on.

Practised putting William in the trailer by putting Midi in first and then taking her out. He was quite good about it and didn't load too badly on Wednesday morning for his third appointment. Not sure how he will get on with his last one, I think he will have to go for a jolly with Mid before that. Tried Midi's rug on him and he was a bit snorty when I first put it on but was quite happy and looked proud with it on. Kept it on for a while then took it off. He looks as if he has dropped weight so I think he will need to be rugged.

Charlotte and Midi after Midi had a full clip and bath – check the tongue out!

March

Found a dead rat in Wills' stable on Sunday and another one in Ben's stable on Tuesday. I thought something was amiss because Wills had chucked his water bucket about. I reckon it went into his stable first of all. The poison obviously works. Not a nice sight first thing in the morning though. The two little dogs came back yesterday from running around the field looking very proud and dirty! They had obviously been down some sort of hole. No kisses or hugs for Tigger today.

Put them all in early and gave Wills the run of his stable as well as the middle bit. He saw a little puddle, splashed in it and was going to roll. I had to shut him in his stable. He seems to have an obsession with puddles.

Survived yesterday and the vet's again. We practised putting William in with Midi on Tuesday night, then took her out. Did that yesterday morning too, so he loaded quite quickly. Teddy was very distressed with William's shouting and was cantering round the inside of his box! Anyway he was great loading coming back, thank goodness. They thought he was so cute at the veterinary hospital. He can be a little monster though.

Had another one of those manic days: got up before six and did the horses (mucked out all four), changed the gate on the field (leccy fencing), went to the garage on the way home to drop off my truck to get it sorted and pick up a courtesy car and guess what? They said the sales team don't come in till 8.30, so my car wasn't ready for pick up. Muttered out loud, filled in paperwork, went home, took boss's dog for a walk (have her till Friday), got home, went to have a shower, son was in shower, argh! Paced up and down till he came out, got showered, went back to the garage, swapped cars (got a Ford Fusion), went back home, picked up dog and took her to work (she comes in every day, she is a very, very large poodle called Milly). Eventually got to work at 9.30 (start at 9), had breakfast and am knackered.

The sarcoid on William's front is weeping a bit so phoned the vet and asked about it. Should it do that, does the cream still have to be put on? I explained to the vet that nobody had actually told me what the sarcoid would do once the cream had been applied. He said the idea is that it should scab then fall off. Still not sure if that is what it is doing, but have stopped the cream and the weeping has stopped. If Will thinks you are going to touch it he tries to bite and knee you.

Went to the ex-racers training day at Brackenhurst College. Boys had great fun jumping. The teacher was, well... er... interesting... Ann just looked at me and said, 'Not being funny but I don't think we will learn anything new here.'

Was putting the tiny terrors out and Midi had that look in her eye. I turned them round and let her go and she tried to sneak back to the gate. I walked in front of her to bar her way and she sort of looked at the water bucket. I thought, *You're going to try and leg it out to the good grass*, so put her head collar back on and shut the gate, let them go and she walked off in a huff.

William is getting better at letting you look at the dodgy sarcoid as he knows you are not going to wash it or touch it.

Tuesday, 13 March

Leant over William today. Ann held him and I stood on the grooming box and put my weight over him. Apart from looking shocked he was OK. I did it a few times and he gave me funny looks but was OK once he was given a few carrots. He is still approx 14.1 hh. on his bum but not quite 14 hh. at his withers.

Ann and I rode out and as usual when we cantered we decided who would go in front. This time I did and off we went. Ben nearly stopped twice at two scary things, but went well. I was just pulling him up in front of the bird scarer, looked round and saw Ann and Teddy lying in the ditch! He had been faffing around, went sideways and his back legs slid down, closely followed by the rest of him and Ann. He was lying on top of her and tried to get up, slid, then when she shouted, 'Teddy get off me,' he got up. She was a bit battered and bruised, and covered from head to toe in mud but thankfully was OK. Teddy was shocked and in bits but seemed OK apart from a few minor scratches. Ann had hurt her leg and we were quite a bit away from home so I told her to ride Ben and I would get on Ted. I got on him and he started faffing again so I walked him all the way home. He was grinding his teeth and pulling, what a palaver. Stuart, Ann's husband, came and took Ann to casualty while I sorted out the horses and put them to bed. Sarah came out and gave me a hand and Paul said that we could have phoned them and someone would have come up the track and got us in the truck – how kind and nice to know. After Ann's check-up she was told she had bruised ribs, her ankle is swollen and she has a sore knee and lots of bruising – but she is so lucky. She is going to be measured for a new type of back protector which saves you from being crushed but weighs half a stone. I want to get one too!

Teddy is a bit depressed and hasn't been eating properly so Ann has to ride him sooner than later. I managed to talk her out of doing the one-day event in April as it is now mid-March.

We aimed to go and get some more straw from another source but that was put on hold by Ann's injuries and the lack of truck!

Charlotte has been on the lunge again on Midi and Midi, bless, even cantered a few strides for her. She really does give 101 percent. She looks after Charlotte when she is riding now. I am sure there will be times when she will say, 'Enough is enough,' but at the moment she is a superstar.

Went into William's stable after he was put to bed with the head collar and he legged it to the back of the box, he probably thought I was going to sit on him again!

Have started riding in the fields now due to the drier weather and Ben is pinging. We put a jump up in the field and the mob had to come and have a look and a snort. Midi trotted over the poles and William sniffed and had to touch them with his hooves. The big boys just looked and went off again.

I jumped Ben and he was doing well, but then knocked it down so I had to get off and put it up again. I was just going to get on and he hugged into my arms. I told him I was still going to ride him even if he did hug me! He shut his eyes and had forty winks. I think he was saying sorry for knocking down the jump.

Bought another rug for William, a half-neck, medium-weight one for the bargain price of £25. We tried it on him and he was spinning round and round when I tried to do the back-leg pieces up. Eventually he cottoned on and accepted it.

Got more straw delivered. I'm taking up knitting, it is much easier.

Sunday, 18 March

The wind has turned bitterly cold after a week of lovely warm weather so put William's rug on (the thin, full-neck one) and put him out in the field. He is starting to moult and since I am allergic to horsehair thought it would be a good idea to put the thin rug on to keep the evil wind off him and also to help shed his winter coat. At first, he fiddled a bit with the front straps but then proudly walked out with Midi. They saw the full jump up in the field and he had to canter round to look at it suspiciously. Midi looked, then ate. Put the big boys out, who immediately had to inspect William and his rug in case he was a stranger. Why do they think it is someone else when they have a rug on? Surely they must smell the same. They pestered him for about twenty minutes and then settled down.

Tessa has been bothering the horses again, but knows she has done something wrong when I chastise her. Paul shut her in this morning because she was at it again. Teddy came in yesterday with a twisted shoe, probably because he was running round the field.

Tuesday, 20 March

The weather was really bad, you could see it coming across the hills; big black clouds. The mob were glad they were coming in and rushed to us. William has his new, thicker half-neck rug on today and he survived the night with jammies on, bless, I am sure he feels better when he is warmer. The thinking is that if he doesn't use his energy to keep himself warm he will grow! Ann measured his bum and it was 14.2 hh., I think he has had a growth spurt!

Teddy still has a face on and won't eat his breakfast in the mornings. The new hay we got is rubbish – literally full of rubbish. Phoned Alex to tell him and he is bringing another bale to try.

Went to Surrey to look at a youngster for Ann. He is from Catherston Dazzler. Well, we trundled down the M1, then the M25, which is commonly known as the biggest car park in the UK and got there three hours later. He is a little sweetie and about 15 hh. at the moment; Ann managed to get him for £1,400 with rugs. He loaded tentatively, bless, but went on and just ate all the way home. The TomTom navigation system was getting a bit above itself on the way home; we got a wrong number on the phone and it was answering it even though Ann said not to. I told Ann to switch it off before it took over and drove the car.

I drove the last part home and the new youngster travelled beautifully with Ben's travel rug on and hadn't sweated. It definitely is in the breeding! Put him out with the mob and they had a little run round. I had asked Ben not to bully him and he was so good and didn't.

We were all standing there, watching, and I said that Ben was probably saying in his Irish accent, 'Oi, I tink we have a new one here.' Midi will have said, 'Eeh, me duck, you'll be OK.' William will have said, 'Awright, Taffy.' Teddy, slightly poshly, will have said, 'Oh, you are the new person.' We reckon Daz talks poshly too and would have said, 'Well actually, I don't run round being silly, I float.' (He did float when he trotted.)

Dazzey's only problem is that he windsucks at feed time or if he is a bit stressed so will have to try and chill him out. He has the stable next to Teddy.

Put the little 'uns out first, then Daz, then the big boys. They were so good with him and apparently later on William and Daz were playing. I am so pleased as it will be nice for the two young 'uns to have a mate each! Dazzey is still slightly dazed with it all but seems to have settled fine and no one seems to be picking on him.

Midi is still a bit wheezy so I have told Ann that when Daz goes for his jab, she should get Midi checked out. She feels so sorry for herself.

The weather has turned very cold and windy again so thought it best not to ride the boys.

Had more trials and tribulations with my truck and OH has

negotiated a full check with Nissan, basically, if they say it is OK then I shut me gob! I can live with that.

Saturday, 24 March

Ben and Ted had swapped stables during the night. The connecting door must not have been shut properly and since Ben can open doors… So there was Teddy looking over Ben's door this morning and Ben in Teddy's stable talking to Dazzey.

Put them all out and William and Dazzey were both eating a little bit, then they were playing and rearing up and Dazzey put his front legs on William! William's leg strap came undone and would he let me do it? No. I had to go and get a head collar and hold him to do it.

> *Lesson*: if you want to do something in the field with the horse take a head collar.

Lots of hay was left overnight, nobody seems to like it but the sheep. What expensive hay!

Dazzey has really settled in after only two days and socialises with them all, well, all except Midi because she just eats.

The mob got out. A part of the leccy fencing was down from the previous adventure and Midi popped over, followed by the rest. Ben, Midi and Wills went next door and were munching the lawn. The other two just raced up and down the fence. You can see who has the brains! Sarah and Paul rounded them up, sorted the fence and put them back in.

Wednesday is coming up and William has another hospital visit. Hopefully he will go in the trailer.

Dazzey has settled in well, but he is going to be one of those kids who are always skinning their knees. He came in with a cut on his knee, funnily enough it matches the scar on his other one!

Took William to the hospital for his injection above his eye. The vet says he is two and a half and will be three in the summer going by his teeth. He was a late baby, bless, and not as old as I thought.

He loaded second time this morning with a bridle on, but would he go in on the way home? Oh no! He was a pain and was a bit sleepy because he wasn't done till late and would have just stood on the ramp all night. Eventually, when he decided that we thought it was his idea, he went in.

Put him out when we got home and Dazzey's face was a picture. He was strutting around, looking at Wills – he thought he was a strange horse because he had only seen him with his rug on before. They must have all had a hoo-ha round the field because when brought in guess who had cuts? Dazzey had a cut above his lip, a lovely big skinned bit on his back and his knee was like a balloon. He threw a complete strop when I tried to clean it. Ann can't do it because her ribs are still hurting and she wears a back protector when handling him because he is still a bit pushy. We ended up Purple Spraying the back and I put some cream on his knee and lip. He was really mardy by the time he went to bed and windsucked everywhere. It is definitely a stress thing.

Thursday, 29 March

Sheep have gone out to the fields on the hill and the chap who owns them said to me this morning, 'What a lovely sight, eh? All those sheep dotted in the field?' 'Nah,' I said, 'field looks as if it has measles.' Having problems getting hay the horses like. Bought one from Buttercup Feeds and they don't like that, got another one from The Clothes Horse, nope, don't like that. Alex is going to get us another one to try, spoilt brats or what!

Went out to get the mob with Ann and Charlotte. When I shouted Dazzey came, so then went to get Ben. They were all caught except Wills and he came over for a carrot. I was just about to put his head collar on and he turned away from me and legged it. He kicked out on the way past and got me on the leg. Not sure what is wrong with him, if he starts doing that he is on the way out. I am afraid I don't do ungrateful horses!

Went to get the mob in on Thursday, shouted at William and he came trotting up to me, all lovey-dovey. Reckon the big boys had a word with him. They probably said, 'Do that again and you are on your way out, mate.'

Dazzey bit Ann on the back when she was putting them out on Saturday morning. She took William and Dazzey and Charlotte took Midi. I had a lie-in because we went to the opening of our local pub after it got a new landlord. Feels too much like a wine bar now – not cosy. We did tell him all the things we didn't really like, including having no crisps or nuts for sale! You have to have crisps and nuts!

Put the jumps out in the back paddock. Paul put a trailer on the back of his truck and took them out for us. The paddock is nice and springy at the moment. Midi might have to go in there soon as she is a chunky, porky, little person. Jumped Ben and Ted, Ben was a superstar. Got some more hay and straw from Alex as we are too knackered to go and get our own now.

Ann and I went to an evening of eventing at Arena UK. They had dressage, cross country and showjumping demos and it was very enjoyable, especially the showjumping demo. Oliver Towend was a laugh and even got on one of the horses at the end and jumped it while talking into a hand-held mike.

Jumped Ben and Ted again and Ben, bless, is being a little star. Ann has someone coming on Monday morning to show her a new feed additive for windsucking, so we will see if it works.

Midi was kept in until three and all the boys hung round the gate till she went out. Paul and Sarah said that every time someone looked at her she whinnied. The babies were happy to wander off with her when she went out eventually.

Dazzey was being evil when we went to catch them and had a go at William over the food. None of the others ever do that and will happily share. We think it might be to do with the wind-sucking, which can be caused by too much gut acid. He even had an evil face on at feed time.

Ann bought the very expensive tub of stuff for Dazzey, ahem, £80, so fingers crossed it will work. Midi was really wheezy this morning after only being out for an hour. I told Ann to phone the vet as Dazzey needs his second jab anyway. As I thought, she has an allergy to something out there and has to stay in and lose weight! Bless her, poor little starving pony!

Midi has been in for a couple of days and apparently has turned into a bit of a hooligan on the lunge. Ann lunged her before Charlotte rode and she was bucking and stopping and she also pinged really high over a jump. When Charlotte got on she jogged down the road. Wonder if it is the steroid jab she got? Whatever it was she felt really good.

Left William in his stable with the bit in-between open so he could wander, Midi was out in the communal area and Dazzey was in his stable. When we came back from jumping William was out talking to Dazzey and Midi was in his stable. Don't know who opened the gate.

The boys were pinging. We put up a grid and they were racing down it. Ben had one stop when we put in an oxer but went OK after that. We were going sideways and everything, he was really full of enthusiasm. Wonder if it is the spring sunshine? The paddock at the back is great for jumping, you just have to make sure you don't go down the bottom when someone is teeing off as it is right next to the Golf Course and you periodically hear a twack!

Sarah is looking for another horse so here we go again!

We put Midi out in the back paddock for an hour but the midges started to bug her. I jumped on her and promptly hurt my rib again. (Did it initially when backing William.) Gave Ann a lesson and had to remind her about her wrists, which she tends to cock when riding. Teddy is really attacking his fences and going well.

April

Easter Monday Morning

Midi finally managed to escape. I tried to stop her but she can't half shift. She ran right down the road to the boys, who promptly barged the fence and jumped into the big bit of the field. Would Midi be caught? Oh no. Ann had to run right down past the neighbouring house and chase her back, she just kept wanting to eat the good grass. Charlotte brought me a scoop with some nuts and she came to me when she was chased back down the road. Dazzey was the only one who wouldn't jump out so we had to bring him in with Midi because he was getting a bit upset. The boys were happy to be caught and put back into their own field. Never a dull moment.

Noticed Wills doesn't like strangers and is very shy around them. He was a bit funny with Sarah's son and his girlfriend. I am sure that is why he was funny the day he kicked out.

Some of the hay is totally crap again and we are finding lots of rubbish in it. Midi is eating it though because she is still confined to barracks. Ann has been lungeing her and she jumped three feet over a jump though she is not reducing in size at all! Have been giving Ann lessons and she is improving slightly and not cocking her wrists as much. The babies just play and play and play, which is lovely to watch.

Am off to the New Forest for two days with OH and will pick Myson up on the way back. Must remember to tell the boys I am going.

Had a nice, quiet time at the New Forest, saw lots of trees and ponies. Boys were fine while I was away.

On Sunday morning Ann's friend brought her harness over to try on Midi. What a superstar Midi is, she was tacked up and off she went. We all had a go and bless, what good fun it is, can't wait till Ann gets a little cart. I took her and pushed her bum to make her trot!

Sarah got her horse on Sunday, she went all the way to Wales, to a place near where William came from! His name is Bailey, he is about 15 hh. a Welsh cross and he is so sweet. We put him out in the field with the mob and they all just looked, had a little run round and ate! We couldn't get over it and sort of said, 'Oh, is that it?'

Dazzey and William continue to play and play and they have now started to play with Bailey. This morning I took Midi out for a bit of grass and Wills and Bailey came cantering across to see what was what. Charlotte was riding Midi on her own in the little bit between the stables and she even got up to a little trot. I ran behind her and pushed her bum again and she kept trotting. Rode Ben with just a head collar on and he was so good, we even had a jump. It is good for your nerves and makes you ride with your seat and your aids – and it is also great fun.

There is a charity ride at Milton Keynes in June that I think we are all going to go to, where you can go over the jumps on the cross-country course as well. Wills has his last (hopefully) hospital appointment tomorrow so I hope he loads OK.

Took my little fat princess out for grass next to the boys' field and William and his new mate Bailey came trotting up as a pair, wondering who she was. Duh! William was thinking about biting the fence so had to shoo him off.

William was a good little man going into the trailer, he was a bit stubborn but was enticed in with some nuts rattling in the feed scoop. My little princess was of course in the trailer first, eating hay. The vet hopes that will be William's last visit and they are really pleased with the sarcoids, especially the one above the eye. She has been taking pictures of each treatment and says it looks good, fingers crossed. He loaded quite nicely on the way back, again first being stubborn, then enticed with food. He had been sitting on the back bar on the way home and we could see him swaying through the window, bless, he is a good boy.

Put him out with the others while we mucked out and he was reluctant to come in and walked away from me when I went to get him. He did let me catch him though after I put Dazzey in (the big boys were all in by then). Dazzey is still windsucking and Ann is going to ask for her money back off the rep who sold the stuff to her. It doesn't seem to be making any difference at all.

Poor Charlotte had her foot stood on by Midi twice, which resulted in her falling out with her and wanting a rabbit. Midi is still wheezy and I think she needs to see the vet again.

William always has to be the one who comes to look at anything strange. Took Midi out for grass again in the morning and William just had to come up and see who it was. He is a little toerag in the field and will bite the electric fence to see if it is on. Charlotte was playing in the paddock with the big black bit of plastic we use to put under the jumps to look like a ditch. She was flapping it around and sitting on it and Ben was a little horrified. I took him near to look at it and he was on the verge of hysteria. However, after perseverance and a few backward movements I managed to get him over it. He dropped a leg and touched it which made him jump up in the air – what a wuss! He did go over it quite confidently at the end though. Good education for him.

Went to the horse market and there was a thoroughbred there which was heartbreaking to see, it looked as if it had a serious injury to its face and its legs had all sorts of injuries. It broke my heart and I just wanted to bring it home. Our lot don't know how lucky they are. Bought a new bridle for a tenner, some travel boots for Wills for nine quid and some mountain rider boots with steel toe caps for Charlotte for nine quid – great bargains.

Rode out with Ann and Sarah past the ditch Ann fell in. Teddy was very good since at the top of the hill we had just passed the bird scarer when it went off. Bird scarers are set by a timer and periodically go off with a very loud bang, which sounds like a deafening gun shot, this scares birds and any other person or animal in the near proximity. We each had a canter down one track and back and they were all strong. Coming back up the track Teddy started to faff about so Ann shouted at him and sorted him out, so then Ben started – what a prat. We all got back in one piece thank goodness and then had a jump.

William came in absolutely filthy on his legs. He had been in the muddy wet bit of the field, which is fenced off because the pipe is leaking under the surface. It is all wet and oily there and guess who had to play in it, get caught in the electric fence and pull it all down? Yes, Wills. He was funny getting caught though, because he frightened himself.

Have started seriously to up the XC prep for our first competition in two weeks' time. Ben is really pinging! Took him out yesterday and there was a new water trough in the sheep's field, well would he go past it? No way. Had to reverse right up to it then turn him round and then he whizzed past it. What a numpty. The worry was the ditch at the side of the road, that is, in case he backed into it. Bought some more hay at £2 a bale. Sarah has got fifty and we have fifty. Still have to get into gear and go and fetch our last load of hay from our old yard.

Charlotte had her new boots on and keeps asking everybody to stand on her toes! She did quite a lot of cantering today as well, the weight of the boots probably helps to keep her on.

Tuesday, 24 April

Took Wills round to the paddock with his bridle on, he looked as if he was going to be sick until he saw new things to look at and then he shut his mouth. He trotted round happily with me leading him and popped over Charlotte's tiny jumps. On the first one he jumped really high then after that he just jumped a tiny bit. He is one switched-on cookie.

Took Ben back down the road past the monster of a water trough. I never knew you could trot backwards, anyway, after a slap and a bit of verbal from me he went past it. Ann has been throwing a wobbly with Teddy, I think because she is tired, and has threatened to sell him and Charlotte on eBay! She had been backchatting so didn't get to ride. Have been taking Midi out for grass in the morning if I have time. She is a tiny terror and tries to drag you off down the road. Was in a bad mood this morning and mucked out all five – not just skipped out, but mucked out and put new straw in! Have put the hanging snaffle bit back in Ben which is good for canter work but not trotting and flat work because he is leaning on the bit, will have to put the Myler back in for flat work. Have got to get the money off Ann for the straw we got on Saturday as well as this hay.

Went XC training with Ann to Aylesford. My heart wasn't in it and we were c★★p at first and Ann wasn't jumping much either.

After we had been doing it a bit we both got our nerve up and the boys were pinging! I jumped the chair, hurrah! We really needed to do it before next weekend. Charlotte was jumping in the back paddock and Midi put in a big one. Did Charlotte look the biz or what? Might not take up knitting just yet.

Wills has taken to playing in puddles again, he had a splash and a play on the way back from the field again. Am a bit worried about Dazzey, he looks as if he has wobblers syndrome. Ann is having the back lady out to look at Teddy so she will take a look at Dazzey as well.

Ben is turning into a bit of a hooligan when I am doing my XC training with Teddy. He goes sideways and prances and wants to race! Next XC is in June. Midi is in because she is still too porky and so Dazzey has someone to talk to if need be. Mind you, he is behind bars so that he can't windsuck and he is also on shavings so that he doesn't eat the straw. He eats every scrap of hay at night.

May

Dazzey is still confined to his stable as we await the vet to refer him. We take William and Midi over to have a groom which seems to cheer him up. He is still on rubbish hay. Midi is still wheezy so gave her three antihistamines this morning, hopefully that will help.

Went to Eland Lodge cross country. Ben was looking at everything and shied at the grass, the gravel, a tree, a dandelion… anything that looked dodgy. He jumped everything though, except the ditch. He just dug his heels in and wouldn't go near it, so we were eliminated. We would have been placed because we had the nearest optimum time! Teddy was fifteenth out of about fifty-seven and went clear, bless, he was a sweetie.

Our front field has been altered and the mob went into the small paddock at the back. We asked Paul if we could build a ditch and hey presto, when we went up there on bank holiday Monday there was a lovely freshly dug ditch! Just have to shore up the sides now and make it how we want it.

Ann and I have been talking about a lorry, we would love one, just got to convince the men.

William has learned that the leccy fence is not on and leans on it to get at the good grass! Ann is a bit concerned about Dazzey and his wobbly legs and is going to get Georgina, the vet, to look at him when she comes to see Teddy. If Dazzey doesn't want to play Wills goes and bites Teddy and gets him to play.

Charlotte got first prize on Sunday in lead-rein class. She was the only one in it but that doesn't matter. Have to look for a second-hand outfit for her now!

The vet came out to Dazzey just as he nearly fell over. He said he thought it was wobblers and to starve him for six months and hope that the bones in the neck grow off the nerve. Said the only way to confirm the diagnosis is to X-ray, so Ann arranged to take him up to the veterinary hospital. We went and they did the X-ray and said yes, it was wobblers and there was nothing they could do as the vertebrae were fused at various parts of the neck. Ann was in tears and we duly took him home. She had phoned the surgeon at Liphook previously and he phoned her back and she told him what they had said at our vet's. He said he'd like to look at the X-rays to see if he could operate. What a hoo-ha to get our vet to email them! Our vet said they had a meeting and all decided nothing could be done, Ann had to keep phoning them to get them to send the X-rays. The surgeon said he would like to operate and Dazzey has a fifty–fifty chance. Trying to get him referred was a nightmare and took Ann a lot of phone calls. It seems as if they had decided nothing could be done, but we think he deserves a chance so on 5 June we are taking him down. Funnily enough it will be four years since Ben had his op; spooky!

William was scratching his ears on a beam above his head in his stable. I wondered what he was doing wobbling his head and then saw his ears touching the beam. Dazzey hasn't been out with him so he has to play with Teddy and Bailey. He tried to play with Ben too, but Ben wouldn't join in.

After a long dry spell we have had a lot of rain and William is pleased because he likes to have a splash in any available puddles. I let him go in the one in the yard when he comes in at night. He just plays and plays out in the field and still runs everywhere rather than walking.

William has been funny about being caught, not sure what is wrong with him. He is being funny about his head collar in particular. Have started leaving it on him for a bit longer. Spent a weekend sorting the ditch out and getting Ben over it. We tried lungeing him over it, chasing him; no chance. I had to get on him and take a lead from Teddy. You could see the light bulb switch on and he sorts of stepped over it. I had to smack him and shout at him a few times but he did it eventually. He is not talking to me now and is jealous of William as well because I have started to do a bit of work on the lunge with him. I showed him the ditch and he snorted and tentatively stepped up to it and played in the muck.

Was putting Ben and Wills out one morning and after I tied William up outside the stable I went in to Ben, took his rug off and he shoved the door open, walked out over the road and into the field. He shouted at William as if to say, 'Are you coming?' The next day he tried to do it again and walked out of the stable, but I put him back in and gave him trouble.

Will is still standing on his bucket in the morning and trying to squash it. He finishes his feed and then stands on it and paws it and pulls it round the box, not sure what he is trying to say.

Ben has been jumping the ditch every day, well not jumping exactly, he hasn't quite grasped what to do, he goes sort of, flat, over it. Put a pole over it to help but he goes just the same. Midi jumped it and pinged over it, she also jumped one of the big jumps again, what a superstar. She really tucks her legs up when jumping. Gave Ann a bit of a flat lesson as she has her first affiliated ODE on Tuesday. I am at work and can't really afford any more time off for non-holidays. Been giving Midi four antihistamines a day and it seems to be helping her.

Went XC training to Aylesford again and Ben was a superstar, he did the ditch and everything with a ditch under it. He would go up to it, look at it, go, 'Oh, I can do the ditch,' and jump it, nearly from a standstill. I am so proud of him and if he goes that well next Sunday I will be over the moon. Teddy lost a shoe so we phoned the farrier while on the course. Being bank holiday weekend we didn't hold out any hope. He was going to try and come on Saturday night but was too late shoeing in Leicester. Anyway, Ann phoned Stuart's mate who is a farrier, but he was going on holiday on Monday so couldn't come but gave Ann the duty farrier in camp's number. He is going to come at lunchtime on Monday. Failing that she will take him to the ODE on Monday and get the farrier there to put the shoe on so she can still do her ODE on Tuesday.

Been looking at lorries and am still swithering as my truck has gone into the garage yet again.

Had another one of those days: I went to the yard and my brakes felt a bit odd. Anyway, drove carefully there and applied my brakes outside the yard and didn't think I was going to stop! I thought I would have to pull the handbrake up. As is usual with these things, it was a Saturday afternoon and the garage was shut so I phoned the AA. A lovely mechanic came out and came for a drive with me and the brakes seemed to be fine but as I got to the yard and braked they made an awful noise and it clunked when I reversed. 'Oops,' he said, 'I see what you mean.' He cleaned the front brakes and advised I take it to the garage as he said he thought the ABS had gone.

Monday morning, off I went to the garage. I explained my problem and they said they would try and find a car for me. They didn't think they would have one and said I would have to wait till the sales team came in so I could get one of theirs. I suggested I take my car to work, wait for the brakes to go while driving and then get the AA to recover me to the garage (I was fed up waiting). They said no, no and got me a car. Mine was taken to Nissan and the person who drove it said it felt like the ABS was kicking in. I phoned the garage, spoke to them and told them that was not the case and the brakes had failed. I was worried they would have a quick drive, say they were OK and give it back to me. I did tell them they would be liable if they said they were fine and then they failed. Turns out the ABS had gone. They ordered a new part and when it came it was the wrong part so here I was with a Fiesta over the bank holiday weekend so Ann had to tow to Aylesford XC for practice. Should get the car back on Tuesday, have also asked them to check the clunk. I told OH that if anything else goes wrong I have had it and will get rid of it... erm, I could get a lorry and a little car?

When we walked the ODE course on the Monday (bank holiday) Ann asked the farrier there if he could put the shoe back on on the Tuesday morning and he said yes.

Tuesday, 29 May – the day of the ODE.

When Ted was doing the dressage he could hear the tannoy system and it hyped him up. Ann made a mistake with the test but it wasn't a total disaster. The showjumping, well, he had to wait around in the ring until the jumps from the previous person were put up, the guy had a cricket score and his little coloured just wouldn't jump. Teddy stopped at a downhill double, we think because the sun was shining on the filler, but jumped it the second time. He had another two down but not bad for Ted. XC, well, what a superstar! He pinged round everything and Ann let him go on a bit for a change. He respects the bigger jumps and the heavy going didn't put him off, he was just amazing and definitely not outclassed! Now she just has to work on the flat work… methinks we have been there before!

On another note, Charlotte has been on and on about a rabbit and we have all said no, because she already has a pony. Then what turns up in their garden but a baby rabbit from two doors down, apparently the neighbours' bunny had babies and this one escaped. It took them hours to catch it and they brought it indoors as it was eating all their vegetables. The neighbour wouldn't answer the door when they went so baby bunny is staying with them for now. Looks as if Charlotte might end up getting a rabbit after all! God does work in mysterious ways!

Practising in the back field, I jumped Ben over the ditch which by now had water in it, and what a palaver! We had to jump Midi over first and then he followed. He just doesn't trust me 100 percent yet.

Entered Eland Lodge XC. Ben has had a face on since Saturday as he obviously didn't want to go. He went out and rolled about and was absolutely minging. Let Ben share some of my breakfast before we went to the XC, he had some Special K with cinnamon and milk – but it didn't make any difference! A nail from his front shoe had gone down and was sticking up the side of his shoe. Phoned the farrier who said to just take it off. Anyway checked Ben's feet before leaving the yard on Saturday morning and they were all fine. Walked the course, came back, got boys in and Ben had a shoe missing. Phoned the farrier who said he would come first thing on Sunday morning.

June

Sunday, 3 June (Morning)

Hitched the trailer and parked it on the yard, Ben had an even bigger face on and when I got his head collar to get him out, he legged it to the back of the box. The farrier was putting the shoe on and would he stand still? Oh no. Tied him up beside Ted and he scraped the ground with his foot, wouldn't stand still and basically was a pain in the bum. Loaded them and off we went; Ben stamped and pawed all the way there. Got them off and knew we would either be brill or complete c★★p. Warmed up and set off, first two – no problem. For the third one I counted the strides down for him: three, two, one, hup. Did he hup? Oh no. He stopped dead and had his head over the hedge with me sitting on his neck, he then turned round and cantered back towards the start with me on his neck, oops! Pulled his reins and stopped him as I was determined not to fall off and be eliminated. He stopped and I sort of shuffled back onto the saddle, turned him round and jumped the jump. How I stayed on I do not know. He was a pain and had a few stops, I had to put the whip upright and smack him on the last stride before he jumped, which I don't really like doing. We got to the ditch and guess what, he stopped again so I went round to the alternative – a small ditch you could have walked through. He stopped and I wouldn't let him go away from it so he jumped from a standstill. Finished with a grand total of 276 penalty points, but we didn't get eliminated. I was absolutely exhausted. Haven't got a clue what is wrong with him, maybe he had a twinge in his foot. I really wanted to tie him up to someone else's trailer and go home as I was absolutely gutted. I have put the work in, he was fit, I am fit, we dug a ditch, have been jumping 2'9" at home and he has already been round the course, so apart from getting another horse I don't know what to do!

Wednesday, 6 June

William still plays with his bucket in the morning; stands on it and paws it. He and Bailey were on their own in the field and Paul was working in it. Of course William had to supervise. He is so nosey and always has to go and see anything strange. Ann came into the field with her shorts on and he was horrified. He obviously didn't know people have white legs.

Dazzey keeps pushing through his chain on the door and wandering round to the feed room. After the XC on the Monday he did it to me in the morning; he walked round to Wills' stable and was trying to windsuck on the gate. When I went to get him off his mouth was riveted to the gate, trying to get him off was difficult, he was desperate to windsuck.

Took Dazzey to Liphook, left just after 9.30 a.m. as there was a problem on the roads at the Hobby Horse roundabout. Got there half an hour late but were seen quickly. The surgeon did a thorough examination and said yes, it was wobblers. He said it was Hobson's choice in regards to operating. He took X-rays and Dazzey also has a fracture on his neck, which isn't causing the problem. He is hoping that the nerve is just being pinched at one spot and he can then operate and put in a basket to keep the disc off the nerve. Today they were going to inject a dye under general anaesthetic to see exactly what is going on – fingers crossed. Didn't get home till 9.45 p.m. Sarah, bless, phoned me and asked if we wanted the horses bringing in which was a great help.

Not looking good about Dazzey. Ann had a phone call to say he had the nerves trapped in three places, one near the fracture. Basically he has a fifty–fifty chance of things going right if he has the op. If he has it the vertebrae could crumble when he is older and he could also have a very stiff neck. Ann asked me what I would do, I told her it was her decision, I couldn't make it for her. Tough one.

Took Ben and Ted down the road in the trailer on Sunday as I wasn't convinced that the grinding noise was coming from the trailer since it had just been serviced. When we unloaded the boys they just looked as if to say, 'What, we are home?'

Friday, 8 June

Took Ben showjumping at Carol's. Ann didn't want to take Ted so Sarah came with Bailey. They were both superstars. Ben jumped everything first time, even the working hunter jumps with the water tray and the stile. Sarah was pleased with Bailey, he was hesitant but very honest. Have booked to go to dressage next Wednesday evening so hopefully the weather will hold up. Ben is being a right pain riding out and is really, really spooky, have changed his feed back to basic nuts with just a handful of competition mix. His feet are awful as well, all cracked and split. I have been putting Vaseline on twice a day as the farrier has suggested. They were like this before, at the Hollies with all the sandy ground.

Sunday, 10 June

Bad news; Ann and Stuart had been talking to Sarah and Paul about Dazzey. Ann made the decision to put him to sleep and the first I knew of it was tonight. Stuart was having a bit of a go about William fighting with him on Saturday and I felt that he was insinuating that his illness was William's fault. Needless to say things are a bit strained at the yard. I think Ann is going to get another horse as she says she doesn't want to buy someone else's problem and now she wants to start again. But as I said to her she doesn't have the time! Who does all the mucking out and putting out? Haven't been doing Ted in the mornings to prove a point and put Midi's bed up as well. She is still wheezy and I think more time and money needs to be spent on her, not another one, argh!

Monday, 11 June

Had a really big fight with Ben, I think being really wound up is affecting my riding. Anyway I really pushed him and tried to get him to listen to me and not look for monsters. Got some nice work but have to change the bit back to the Myler as he doesn't go as well on flat work in the hanging snaffle. Asked Sarah if I could borrow it back, she is going to try Bailey in her hanging snaffle again as she was a bit wary of him but is getting more confident.

Couldn't go to dressage because Ben pulled his shoe off the night before, he was moving away from the killer fly spray and his shoe slipped to the side and was hanging off. Ann put Teddy's swinging toy thing up in Wills' stable, it has a salt lick on it and a ball that has a salt lick in it. Ben was playing with it while waiting to be shod. Wills figured out how to do it as well and joined in. The farrier came late and while Ben was getting shod Wills decided to lie down because it was past his bedtime, well, it was after 7 p.m. Does he have no shame or what?

Ann is talking about looking at a youngster near Doncaster. Our farrier knows the person and the horse and says it is not worth the money and it hasn't been handled much. Will see what she does about it.

Sunday, 17 June

Took William and Midi to a local show in the morning, Charlotte just rode round but I did an in hand one-, two- and three-year-old class. I could tell as soon as I went into the ring that the judges weren't interested as they didn't even look at us. One of the photos says it all: I am trotting and they are looking elsewhere. Dinky little showy things were placed but all said and done Will was a superstar. The only things that really fazed him were the awning set up for people to sit under and the judge's stick, which he kept waving about. He kept playing with the chain on his in-hand bridle. I got it from the horse market for £8. It's all experience for him. He loaded first time going and coming back and didn't poo at all!

Sarah and I did the pairs and came third and we also did the 2'3". I was second and Sarah was fifth with two stops. Ben was a superstar and listened to me and went beautifully. Ann didn't go as the in-laws were visiting.

Teddy has had a shoe missing for a week and is depressed. He has come in from the field with loads of bites, this always seems to happen when he is not working. William is still running everywhere and playing with Teddy.

Rode Ben, did some fast work first then practised my dressage test. Thought I would try faceache over the ditch, would he do it? Oh no. He tried to rear and turn round again so had a bit of a fight and made him go forward. The golfers must have heard some pretty bad language! Popped him over a jump to finish. He was really, really sweaty. I threatened to take him to the market and sell him I was so annoyed. Our farrier is off with cracked ribs after getting kicked by a youngster so another farrier came to do Bailey and Ted. Ted seemed relieved to get his shoes back on. Ben stood in his stable in disgrace.

It has really been tipping it down so it looks like the dressage might be off on Sunday. Would like to have gone showjumping this Friday but don't think that will be on due to the rain as well. Where has the summer gone?

Saturday, 23 June

Rode Will with a saddle, bridle and stirrups and he was a poppet. Got Ann to walk out with me and we went down the road a bit and she got him to trot beside her. I started to do a rising trot and he stopped and looked puzzled. Me rising up and down obviously felt funny to him.

Sunday, 24 June

Went to dressage with Ben and Ann and Teddy. It was a lovely little quiet place over near Barrow. Ben got fourth out of ten and Ann wasn't placed, and had a right face on with Ted. We did clear round showjumping and it was about 2'6"–2'9". Ben had a stop at the double the first time and had two poles down but no stops on the second so he did well. There were scary fillers and everything.

The weather has been really, really wet lately with lots of thunderstorms so I kept the boys in and guess what, it was dry today, argh, typical. It is the wettest it has been for fifty years. Mind you, when you go to the field and rattle the scoop with feed in it they all still come running. The field is so wet Will splashes when he canters round.

William has been cheeky again with Ben, he was nibbling at the back of his rug and pulling it, and then pulling it a bit more until Ben had a playful kick at him as if to say, 'Bog off.' I think he needs to do more work. If he is out in the morning and Teddy comes out afterwards, he goes straight to him and annoys him and wants to play, biting him and rearing. Methinks he has too much energy! He came in and I thought he was going to groom Midi, well then his dingly-dangly came out and I thought he was going to be naughty.

Ben has been Mr Spooky big time and is snorting and shying when out on his own. Don't know what the answer is. I have been putting the Vaseline on his feet night and day to help keep them supple so hopefully that will help. Midi is still wheezy so I got her apple cider vinegar, not sure if it helps as she is wheezy, then not, then wheezy again... Still lots and lots of rain though it dried up on 28 June and wasn't bad at all to ride on. Bad rain is forecast for the weekend and it is the Rearsby show, which I would like to go to.

Was fed up of hacking out so took Ben into the back paddock. It was a bit wet but we jumped over two barrels on their side and then one single one on its side. Ben was a bit funny at first but then did the one on its own.

Bedtime for Will!

July

Tuesday, 3 July

Was going to take Ben showjumping to Vale View but we were waiting for the farrier for Midi and he didn't come. Weather was awful as well so he got a night off. Rode William instead. We followed Sarah on Bailey down the road for about 100 yards and he was as good as gold. He even led some of the way. We got back to the yard and Bailey kept going in the other direction and William wanted to follow. Off we went down that way for a little bit and turned round, Bailey trotted and so did William for quite a few steps – what a star, his first proper trot!

The farrier came in the morning and I got Ben out of the field so he could check his shoes. He put another nail in the front. He was faffing about looking at the others and stood on my right foot, did I swear! Although I did do it quietly because Charlotte was there. I felt sick and dizzy and had to sit down. My big toe is skinned and the toe next to it has gone all black and blue. What a pillock. Was doing everything possible to get Ben ready for 15 July and then I go and get injured.

Rode William. Tacked him up, got on and did up his girth. He just looked at me. We toodled round the little enclosed bit, then he walked up to see Teddy in his stable and then we went out through the feed room to the outside bit. He wanted to go up through the muck to the back paddock and then into the big shed but I managed to turn him round. We went to see Ben in his stable and then William wanted to walk down the road the way we went the other day. I managed to turn him then ride him back through the feed room. He stopped in front of Midi's stable and wouldn't budge so I got off, led him to the stool and then got on again. We went out again and he wanted to go back to the paddock. I turned him round and he saw a bit of grass that made him snort and then he noticed the kitchen window of the house, well, did he stare. He stood for ages trying to figure it out. I think he could see himself or else it was the big pottery pig in the window. At any rate, he was a superstar. I rode him back through the feed room into the little bit at the back and got off and untacked him. When I put him in his stable he yawned and yawned, he was obviously exhausted. He is so inquisitive, which is good. Put him out in the morning and he wanted to play as usual and pestered Teddy then Bailey.

What a start to July. It has been so wet and they are all fed up in the field. Bailey barged through the single-strand gate and the next day all five got out. They know the fence isn't on so they just push at it. Sarah had to get a scoop with nuts and rattle it but once she did they all came no problem, expect for William, who is still a bit suspicious. They lured him with the nuts to the gate and then shooed him in. He had gone over to Midi who had jumped over the gate that separates the bit that she is in from the road. It was about 2'9" and she had her fly rug on but she popped over it and went round the corner and ate the grass. The boys were running up and down the field and then they must have got out.

Ann led Ben in and thought Teddy would just follow but he walked off round the corner to look at the horse trailers then came back round. He obviously just wanted to have a look.

Ann has bought another youngster. WB x TB, he is one year and one month old and he will be picked up after her holidays. He has to be gelded yet and I suggested she booked him in now so he will be done on 23 July.

Have been trying to get somewhere to take Ben jumping before his ODE on 15 July. Everywhere is too wet. Am still a bit worried about his shoes as two nails are really sticking out on the outside of his front foot. Am going to try and get the farrier to come at the end of the week to check them.

Went to the horse market for a look, could have come back with another three! Bought one of the things that you put in the back of the car and put your saddle on. It is pink but that is the only colour they had. Mind you, it can't be seen, so should keep my street cred.

Did a bit of jumping with Ben and Ted. Ben was being casual, Teddy just knocked the jump down, then again and again! Think

I have seen the problem now and can hopefully get it sorted. When we were out I told Ann about working even on a hack. You can canter and bring them right back in hand, do changes, make them trot uphill with their heads down – you can do all sorts to try and keep them going.

Midi is still eating and eating and eating. I have never known a horse to eat so much. She takes Charlotte into the feed room and pushes the lids off the bins and puts her head in. She has no shame.

Charlotte got new wellies from Burnley and they look just like hunter boots. She is tickled pink, wish I still felt the same about a new pair of wellies.

Been riding William for a few days bareback – without a saddle or bridle, only a head collar. He is fine. I get on and off he goes. He is determined to either go to the back paddock or through the muck to the big shed.

The dogs make me laugh, when you are mucking out they sometimes sneak in and lie in the corner of Ben's stable. Tessa will lie there snuggled up to Tigger and look at you with one eye as if to say, 'You're not going to move me are you?' Tigger sometimes comes bouncing in and rubs herself all over the straw and bounds back out again. If you don't talk to them they will come up and talk to you, it is so funny, it sounds as if they are trying to say a word.

Ben's feet are really iffy, with lots of nails starting to stick up. Have text the farrier but am not getting my hopes up. Will be gutted if I can't do the ODE on Sunday.

Teddy seems very depressed and isn't eating much hay or pooing. I think he is sad because Ann is getting a new horse. Mind you, he might be a bit cold so I will put their rugs back on tonight and give him a pep talk to see if that helps.

Ben's feet were awful so text the farrier on Tuesday to come and look, but got no reply so called him, but couldn't get hold of him there either and just felt sorry for myself. On Friday I got a text to say that he was coming at 2.45 p.m. Had to leave work early, rushed to the post office and then up to the yard. Got OH to bring me clothes and wellies. My friend Tracie was coming from Winchester for the weekend and is going to be my groom as

Ann is on holiday, so she met me at the stables. Her sat nav took her to the golf course! The farrier did a great job on Ben's feet and put stuff on them that looked like rubber. Said to coat his feet with really old engine oil and Stockholm tar.

Went to the pub on Friday night for dinner, Saturday afternoon walked the course and then went into the tack shop – which is based at the venue – (bought really expensive jods with a leather seat, a new short-sleeved blouse and good stirrup leathers), cleaned tack, boots, etc., loaded car then went to a BBQ at OH's mate's on Saturday night. Was worried during the night about having to wake up early so got up and set my phone and my watch as well as checking the alarm clock.

Sunday, 15 July

Got up at 4.45 a.m. went to the yard, mucked out, Tracie did Ben and Midi then we set off at 6.30 a.m. Boy, did it rain. Ben didn't do a bad dressage and had four faults and a stop jumping, but not bad for doing it in the rain. I couldn't see as I had tears streaming from my eyes because of the rain! Went XC and nearly took the wrong course but Ben stopped at the drop (which was the wrong jump anyway) and wouldn't jump it. He normally does it first time but he would not go near it again. He reared up and jumped to the side. Somebody shouted that we were going the wrong way and put us right. I reckon my guardian angel was standing there telling Ben not to go down there as we would've been eliminated. Got to the ditch (a small one) and I sat right back, growled and really shoved him, then gave him his head and we did it first time. Tracie was on the hill jumping up and down with glee. She said we could hear her saying well done! We didn't get placed but he was a poppet all day. Loaded first time, came out, went back in, got tacked up in the trailer, rugs on and off in the trailer, an absolute star. He only shouted once or twice – a pathetic little cry for Teddy. Teddy is usually there when he goes XC. I have been threatening him with the 'M' word (Melton Market) if he didn't do it. When I said that to him he just looked at me. What a great day. It would have been nice to have been placed but hey, we weren't eliminated and he has got dodgy legs!

Went out on Sunday to the pub with Tracie, had a great laugh as we always do. She went home Monday morning when I went to the stables. Could do with more laughter like we have when we are together. You really need someone horsey to be your groom at a competition because they know what they are doing. All in all a five-star weekend!

Am swithering about whether to buy a lorry or not. There are lots of pluses and minuses so can't make my mind up. Think I will go with the flow and see what turns up. If it is going to be rainy all the time a lorry would make a great difference.

It's been a year since William first came to us and boy what a year that has been.

Ann is back from her holiday with Charlotte saying, '*gracias*' and '*buenas noches, señorita*' all the time. She rode a camel as well, which she enjoyed.

Ann went with David to pick Eric (the new one) up. He loaded fine with a bit of coaxing and some food and travelled well. He was put out in a separate field with William just so they could get used to one another. They were way, way off down the field and I shouted and rattled the scoop with some nuts and they both came, thank goodness. Put him out with the big boys the next day and they were all fine. They did have a run round as expected but Eric wasn't bullied or anything. He has to go next Monday and have his bits chopped off to make him a gelding. Ann is going to make sure he isn't overfed in case he gets wobblers.

After the ODE things have been a bit flat. The combined training event the following week was cancelled, which I was looking forward to. Mind you, Ben did have a bit of a funny turn and was showing all the signs he had when he was ill before. He was stretching as if to wee and making funny faces. Wasn't sure if it is because Eric is a colt. Anyway I was a bit worried and on Saturday morning, as usual, had to call the vet. Who gets a vet out midweek? I think we only ever call them out at the weekend. He gave Ben a liquid paraffin drench and a painkilling jab to stop his bum hurting. Touch wood he is OK now. He gave me a fright though, I can tell you. Teddy was really worried and kept looking through the mesh that separates them over the door. We had to take it down so he could look over and see that Ben was OK. He was ever so worried, bless!

Eric went to veterinary hospital to have his goolies chopped off, he loaded fine going and coming back and everything went well. The weather has still been so bad, how much rain can you have? They have all, except for Will and Mid, had thin rugs on. Eric has no fat on him to keep him warm so he has William's rug on. Got 100 bales of straw delivered and like everyone else am getting concerned about the hay. It is late July and no hay has been cut because the weather has been so wet. When we eventually can get the hay cut it will be all hands to the pump to get it in… but when though?

Still trying to find a show, ODE or anything at all to compete in. When I can't compete it makes me grumpy and wonder why I have horses! I have all this time because OH is on night shift and have nowhere to go – typical.

Teddy was grooming Eric on first meeting him so he must be a nice chap!

What a tosser Ben was, when bringing them in he went to bite William so I slapped him with the head collar as it was so mean and Will ran off. Well, that set the tone for my ride. We got down the road and he suddenly noticed the white electric fence rolled into a ball, well, was it seriously scary or what? We reared up, went backwards, sideways and cantered backwards but would he go forward? Oh no, it was too scary. The tractor which was cutting the hay then came and did it slow down? Oh no, so he didn't know which way to run. He bounced off the hedge twice and, boy, was I glad there wasn't a ditch or we would have been in it.

We went down the track and there were some killer boulders, then we went sideways, cantering. On the big field beside the road I thought I would do an in-hand canter, well, we did some lovely movements – again going sideways one way then the other, then did a beautiful, full-of-energy trot and some lovely leg yields. But we then got to the scary bit of the electric fence and he stopped dead and spun round, nearly putting us in the barbed-wire fence. Would he go forward? Oh no, not even with a slap. I swore at him big time using the f word a lot and basically telling him he would seriously get us into trouble if he didn't go forward. He then tentatively went past the scary wire. The tractor then came so he jogged and an oncoming van saw us and pulled in, waiting till we passed. He gave me the most 'I feel sorry for you' look. I then took Ben into the field next to the tractor and did a bit of schooling and when the tractor came to the edge of the field I took him near it.

William has been really tidy with his poos, doing them all in the one spot. My baby is growing up now! It has actually been quite dry so had a nice ride out with Ann and Teddy and well, don't you just love a thoroughbred. There is a small hill where I usually go right lead canter, then left, then right and Ben knows this. So what does he do? Goes sideways and does lovely flying changes, what a palaver! Teddy decided to do the same. Typical thoroughbred, think they know it all.

Saturday, 28 July

Rode out on my own in the morning as thought it might rain later. Wore my MP3 player so had music in one ear, boy, did it help pick me up. Ben went beautifully and we were actually moving to the music at some points. Also, you can boogie to some songs while trotting up a hill by leaning forward and getting your horse to put his head down and work from behind. You can sing as well. Must have looked a right sight.

Rode William in the afternoon, he didn't want to go off the yard but didn't mind walking in and out of the stables area. Bailey and Sarah came back and he followed them down the road to meet Ann and Charlotte coming back after a hack. A motorbike passed us slowly and he was so good. Mind you, Ann did tell the driver that there was a young horse up the road and could he go slowly. I even managed to make William trot on my own, he is really on the forehand but coming on nicely. He didn't half yawn when I was finished. I cut his mane as well as he looked really girly. I know you shouldn't cut it but it does look better and he is not a show pony.

Am getting fed up with having no shows to go to and the wet weather so I have my fingers crossed that the ground will dry up now. Shouldn't complain as there are lots of people flooded out.

Rode Ben in the field as the weather was still nice. The chap cutting the hay was walking along the road looking for a bit that had dropped off his machine. That is another day of haymaking lost, I seem to be the only one worried! Ben worked beautifully, I had my MP3 player on again which gives me the oomph to keep going. Ann was getting annoyed with Teddy as he wouldn't work. I got on him and he went lovely, so had to tell Ann what to do again and he did it.

William and Eric getting to know one another on Eric's first day.

August

Saturday, 1 August

Foot and mouth strikes again in Surrey. Paul asked us to only ride on his land and some of the adjoining land so as not to annoy anyone.

Our hay field will hopefully be done on Wednesday and baled at the weekend. Here's hoping. I have calculated that we will need at least 500 bales of hay to keep us going – yikes! Straw is not as bad – I reckon maybe 400 should do it. We are down to our last four bales of hay but Sarah said we could use the twenty or so she has left.

Sunday, 2 August

Ann put Midi out with the mob for an hour. Nobody noticed her for about fifteen minutes then off they went! She squealed because she doesn't like them getting close. She whizzed off round the field with them all following, and boy, can she shift.

Monday, 3 August

William decided Midi belonged to him, his little dingly-dangly was out and he was guarding her. She still squealed if he got close though. Charlotte has gone to her nan's at Taunton for a week so she isn't getting exercised. Ann hogged her mane because she is getting bothered by the flies, she is also wheezy again. Mind you, Ann has stopped giving her the antihistamines.

Ann and I rode round the woods and then went into the cut hayfield. There were some hay bales and loose hay on the floor so we jumped them. We did the pairs a bit but Ben was loopy. I would ask him for canter and he would go sideways one way, then swap legs and go the other way. He is like a little coiled spring, ready to boing! I finally got him to go straight after going about halfway round the field. He is a numpty.

Took Will and Midi for their third jabs, it is cheaper taking them to the vet. Midi was checked for her wheezing and the vet says she has COPD. We are doing all the right things with her to help her wheezing but since they are not working she has to have antibiotics and some more Ventapulmin. Ann is going to fence a bit of the big field for her to rummage in. Worked Ben in the field with my MP3 player on and the boogie music. After fifty minutes I thought I had better stop! Got some nice work from him again so I was very pleased.

William is continuing to be tidy in his box and pooing in the same area, he is not a teenage delinquent after all. OH came up in the morning and reckons his bum is still higher than his withers.

Saw an ODE advertised in the local paper so emailed for the details and I think I will do it. Ann is doing an ODE the same weekend, hopefully on the Sunday and not the Saturday.

Wednesday, 5 August

I was a bit late getting to the yard to take Will and Midi to the vet's so Ann loaded them herself. Midi, of course, went straight on and then William went on with Ann, who had some nuts, then stood while she went round and put the back bar on. What a star!

Thursday, 6 August

Went XC training with Ann and Teddy and Ben was a superstar. I let him have his head and he went a lot better. Ann wants to do the pairs so we had a practice and I just followed them and popped the smaller options. She came to a big jump and we followed and I thought, *Oh s**t*, but just let Ben go. It was only about 3'3"–3'6" and with a big spread of logs! Argh! He was so good, we even went into the water first time while Teddy was a wuss and wouldn't. We had a great time and are going to enter the pairs at Eland Lodge now. Am still buzzing today and can't believe it.

Friday, 7 August

Ben is still suspicious of the water trough, I saw him standing there in the morning; looking at it but not daring to go near. It used to hiss and he is waiting for it to do it again.

Midi was put out into her little paddock and the babies stayed quite close and kept her company. They were both fascinated. Eric had his dingly-dangly out as well, it must be their hormones. Midi just squeals if they sniff over the fence.

Saturday, 8 August

Ann went to fetch Charlotte from the in-laws and the hay was ready to be brought in. Sarah, her sister, Paul, the rest of the family and I started on it. We must have shifted over 500 bales, chucking them onto the trailer. I was absolutely shattered physically. Ann wanted me to ride Teddy but I was too tired.

Sunday, 9 August

I rode Ben and he was a pain and wasn't paying attention to me at all. I ended up swearing at him. He also tripped and went right down onto his nose which really jerked my left hip and leg. Apparently Paul is going to rent out most of the fields for grain next year so we won't be getting hay off the farm and we also won't be able to ride in the fields. Doesn't seem to be much point in stopping there any more as the costs of fuel, etc. don't reflect the facilities on offer. There's no point in travelling a long distance if you can't ride.

William is still playing and playing and started them all off in the field. They whizzed round and reared up and generally mucked around. Midi just ate in her little bit of the field. They whizzed up, showing off to her, but she still just ate. William grooms with her across the electric fence, bless, he does love her to bits.

Monday, 10 August

The plumbers phoned and said could they come tomorrow and put our new central heating in. OH phoned me while I was on the way to the stables and my brain went into overdrive. As a result I put petrol in my diesel car. I shrieked at about seven litres and quickly put the nozzle back into the pump and went in and told them in the kiosk. I could have filled it up and it might still have been OK but don't want to risk it as it is *that* car. I had to be recovered by the AA and taken to the garage to have it flushed out. Thank goodness I didn't start it. I was so embarrassed.

Friday, 14 August

Nothing really happens for a while then *bang* – Ann and I went showjumping to Carol's and Ben, bless, jumped well over a 2'6" course. He got one clear round. Ann had an ODE the next day so put the jumps up higher. Teddy stopped at one and slid into it but cleared it the second time. She came to number ten and he slid into that but didn't recover himself and fell down. Ann was still on him, then he sort of flicked her off, and while he scrabbled round to try and get up, he booted her a few times. There was blood everywhere. I pulled her away from his leg, which was over hers, and he lay there still, for a while. Carol came running over and got her first-aid kit. We decided to call an ambulance as it was Ann's face that was hurt. An ambulance car came in about six minutes and he administered first aid and said she should go to hospital. There were no ambulances available so Carol took her in her car. Her friend came with me because she knew the way to Nottingham and Carol followed. I phoned Paul and Sarah and they came over straight away and got the boys and the trailer and put them all to bed. We got to the hospital about six o'clock and left at ten to twelve. They think her cheekbone is fractured, her elbow is fractured and she had stitches in a wound to her face that goes right through to the inside of her mouth. She has to go back to the fracture clinic on Monday and the maxillofacial unit on Wednesday. She is lucky not to have more injuries, although she says her ribs hurt as well. She has got a really swollen face and a sling on her arm.

Tuesday, 18 August

Ben seems very depressed and didn't want to come in from the field. He is being very clingy to Teddy as well, so not sure what is up with him.

Wednesday, 19 August

After all these happenings I booked a vet's appointment for Teddy, I said I would pay as these casualty visits were getting a bit frequent. We took him up and as Ann had difficulty speaking, I did it all. The vet looked at me when I asked if there was something wrong with Teddy. He asked if he was lame or showing any signs of pain and I said no, but described his episodes of going in the ditch, hitting the deck with Ann on him and generally not being right. I also explained that he had been examined the previous year and had had lots of blood tests because we thought he wasn't right then either. He trotted Teddy up, did the flexion tests and said he was the best he had seen for that age. Not to be put off, I insisted there was something wrong with him and that we wouldn't leave till we found out what. The look I was given was priceless but I wasn't budging. He agreed to X-ray Teddy's back and hocks to see if everything was OK. The X-ray showed that Teddy has kissing spine and he has probably had it for years. Ann cried; I breathed a sigh of relief that there was something and we now know what it is. He was given steroid injections in his spine which the vet said would help and he was to be walked straight for a while and then hopefully everything would be OK. The vet's bill was less than I thought – phew!

Ann won't be going to her second affiliated ODE on Saturday. I don't think she is meant to do it on Teddy! I got to talk to my friend in Walsall who was going to meet us there, so at least something good came out of it.

We are both having thoughts about bringing the youngsters on and are in a bit of a quandary.

Sunday, 23 August

I took Ben to dressage at Rearsby and he was seventh out of seventeen so he did really well and I got two lovely photos taken of us. Ann was going to video me but her tape ran out. The Brooksby area is not a lucky place for her.

Tuesday, 25 August

We have decided to buy a lorry between us! Ann and I went to look at one just outside Loughborough, a Ford Iveco that takes three horses with living. It didn't look too bad and we were interested. I asked her to start it up and it did first time, but as we were talking in the living bit I could smell the diesel fumes – definitely a no-no.

Friday, 28 August

Went down to Northampton where a chap buys and sells lorries from an online business. There was a Mercedes 814 advertised, so off we went to see it. It had loads of living but when you walked round the living it moved from side to side and you felt like you were on a boat. It took three horses as well but just seemed too wide to me. It was started up and you could tell the engine was older because it smoked quite a lot. It was a D reg. He also had an old Bedford and a Leyland Daf which I was interested in. The Leyland Daf looked as if it was an unfinished project and had a brand-new ramp which I could put up myself as it was so light. We were taken for a drive and I really liked it. We went home, talked about it and bought it.

Saturday, 29 August

When we went back down to fetch the lorry we went in David's little automatic so that Ann could drive it back, although she isn't really supposed to drive for another week. Was I nervous or what driving it home? I hit the kerb on the first roundabout, oops, but didn't seem to get on too badly after that. It was getting darker and started to rain a bit so I was a tad nervous, but we got it back OK. A red light kept coming on and I soon figured out that it happened when I went over 50 mph, duh! I'm slightly nervous of driving it until I can figure the gear box out. First and second are funny but the other three are OK. We are going to get it checked out and serviced asap. I know we should have got it checked out beforehand but he sells on the internet and if he was dodgy he will be barred from that site. Fingers crossed everything is OK. Ann has put the trailers up for sale and has had two enquiries for the newer one so fingers crossed for that too.

Sunday, 30 August

Rode Mr Windy Miller (Ben) out round the big straw bales, which are definitely going to bite him. But when I took him up to see one he started to eat it, so don't know what all the fuss is about.

Monday, 31 August

Got the brakes checked out by someone who knows someone who happens to live in the village and knows Kevin at the pub. Apparently the brakes are OK and he had a slip of paper from the rolling road to prove it. But I am not paranoid!

We now have 400 straw and 600 hay bales, so I think we might be staying where we are, imagine trying to store that lot elsewhere!

September

Sunday, 6 September

Well, since we bought the lorry have been busy polishing and painting the inside. It looks better already. I took it to Brooksby for its first official outing. We were travelling down the little road and a car came whizzing round the bend and nearly got us. Got over that and on the way back an ambulance wanted to get past and I had nowhere to pull in, argh! I had an error of course in my dressage and came about ninth, if I hadn't made the mistake we would have been fifth. In the SJ warm-up stakes we were second so we have a lovely blue rosette to go with the lorry. It was lovely to be able to change inside, in the warm. We just need to sort out the gas so we can have a cup of tea. Ann still isn't riding. She tried to go for a walk on Teddy and he started to bounce and play up so she got off. Guess who is riding Teddy now? The farrier came to shoe him but took one shoe off and put it back on as he said there wasn't really enough foot to shoe on. The ground is rock solid so can't really do a lot of schooling as I don't want to wreck their legs.

Tuesday, 8 September

Went on a two-day course with Ginny Patterson to learn how to communicate with horses. I talked to Ben and Teddy by distance, it was really odd.

Friday, 11 September

Am off to Scotland for a few days with Tracey, so hope the boys can cope. William is still playing and playing and playing. When you put the babies out together they start playing before you even let them go. Tried to communicate with the boys while I was away to let them know I was OK, don't know if it worked but they are certainly chilled.

Midi has been in the small paddock for a while and William likes to groom her over the fence. Apparently he has been letting her out. Ann saw him grabbing the electric fence in his teeth, pulling it and then standing on it so that she can get out. Fair play for his ingenuity. Midi's rear end is as big as a house though.

Sunday, 13 September

Rode William and had to get Ann to follow me on foot. He wasn't too keen and got a bit cheeky and tossed his head. The next day I followed Midi with Charlotte riding. I asked him to trot and he tossed his head, I think was trying to buck. He then got stubborn and didn't want to walk so I had to kick him, well, did he have a face on! The next day I lunged him and got him to canter on the left rein but not on the right. The left is obviously his good side. I nearly, but not quite, got carted off and he turned his bum to me in defiance. I had to shout at him quite a bit for being so naughty and then he kept turning in to me so that he wouldn't have to walk forward, what a palaver.

Ann had asked me to do a bit of groundwork with Eric, so got him to follow me and then back up and I touched him all over with the whip and lunge line. He looked completely bemused. I jumped Ben and he is so laid back he is nearly horizontal; the chats with him have been working methinks!

Wednesday, 16 September

The lorry is going in for a service on Monday, I will drop it off Sunday night and take the key round to the guy's house as he lives in our village.

Monday, 21 September

Have had to go to Oakham to work for three days from 3 p.m. till 6 p.m. so I thought I would ride Ben in the morning. The first morning he had a right face on and stomped his feet and walked back and forth so I couldn't put his boots on, then he tried to s★★t on me but he missed – what a to-do! I didn't have a bad ride though, he was on his toes.

The next day Tigger decided to come with me along the road. Tigger runs in and out of the bushes and is definitely a monster.

She appeared at the entrance to one of the fields and Ben was absolutely horrified and spun round and tried to leg it. I shouted at Tigger and Ben and made him go forward with him snorting. What a palaver, he'll never change.

Friday, 26 September

The lorry isn't done and the pump is staying in it. It will cost too much to replace it and it might not make the lorry start any better. The problem is that the engine is addicted to ether. It wants two pumps of the stuff before it starts. I have been trying to wean it off it a bit but to no avail. Our mechanic said the engine is just tired and wants the ether, I said, 'I am tired as well, mate, can I have a can?' He said he would do it on Saturday, but I told him to have the weekend off and do it on Monday.

Saturday, 27 September

Rode out myself this morning and on the way back up the road some killer cows came cantering towards us. Ben saw them over the hedge and was cantering on the spot. I told him to trot on and behave which, bless, he did, then did some hill work, which tired him out.

Sunday, 28 September

Ann was working and I mucked them all out and brought them in while she was riding Teddy. Eric always comes cantering over when you go to catch someone else, he is such a sweetheart. Ben was left in with Midi and, boy, did he squinny because Teddy had gone out and he was left. He could see the babies but that's not the same is it? I shouted Midi over when I had taken Ben in and all I could see was this belly come cantering towards me what a chunk!

Monday, 29 September

They are renewing the water pipe and there is a great big yellow drainage machine at the gate of the field. Had to bring them all in past it, did they notice the big machine? Oh no, they were looking at the coiled-up electric fence! When I put the babies out on Friday we got past the big hole that has been dug and the huge yellow monster but the wind flapped the electric fence and they dragged me towards it. I went splat onto the ground and had to chase them to take their head collars off. Eric was OK but William legged it and turned his bum to me a few times. The rope kept getting wrapped round his leg and he would stand on it, but would he stop? Oh no. I shouted at them when I got them both and they had the decency to look ashamed.

Tuesday, 30 September

Been practising fast work with the boys again and Ben's shoes have started to come loose. You can hear them clinking. The farrier was supposed to come and shoe him on Thursday but text to say that he had flu! He got another one to come, who was very good and came earlier, at 4 p.m. and he was ever so good with Ben. He went round to see all the horses and liked William.

Teddy and William playing with Eric looking on.

October

Friday, 2 October

Went over to Vale View for a lesson. Teddy went the best he ever has gone so his back is obviously feeling better. Ben went well and I was pleased, although he did dump me at the planks the first time. We have sussed out that he likes to put an extra stride in and the teacher doesn't reckon we can change that – but I can live with it. Driving the lorry was weird with two horses in it and you could feel the motion from the top of the lorry on the side that their bums were. Managed to manoeuvre it into the yard OK though, phew.

Sunday, 4 October

Went to Eland Lodge XC, it was great to be able to pack up the lorry on Saturday and just load the horses this morning and leave. Had to go early as I was on at 10.20 a.m. and Ann was at 3.50 p.m. so it was a long day. Great to be able to sit inside and have a cup of tea. The only problem was that although the gas cooker was linked up to the bottle, there was an outlet valve for the fridge with no cap on it, so if you switched it on you got gassed. Bought two taps to put on it but they didn't fit. Have to have a rethink.

Spoke to Ben before we went XC and showed him the course in my mind. He went the best he ever has and only hesitated a few times before he went clear. He was still noseying everywhere but he wasn't really pulling and I finished with lots of energy and a huge yes when I went over the last jump.

Ann got round on Teddy with two stops, she did well to cope with them all. The second to last was a jump over a great big log pile down a hill from out of the woods. She pulled at him a lot but this was because she is still worried and didn't trust him to get on with it. She is adamant she will lose more weight because she was uncomfortable going round and said she couldn't balance properly. Anyway, we all came home safe and sound. Ben was eighth out of forty-three so I was over the moon. Lee's shoes are obviously jumping shoes! Have booked a jumping lesson for next Thursday at 6 p.m.

The weather is changing and they are all getting woolly coats so I am looking for another rug for William and a thicker one for Ben.

Weather has been a bit funny, cold and wet then turning warm. All the mob have wanted to come in because of the flies. Midi comes screaming over to you to come in as she really has a phobia of them.

Monday, 5 October

Got my car swapped and I do miss the truck! Needed to come off the road a bit down the one-way road going to the farm and I could hear the bottom being scraped! My new car is very posh with lots and lots of little controls which you need a degree to work out. Got David on the case. When he was in the car I got him to read the manual for me. We are getting there.

Bought two new rugs for the boys, full-neck ones for when the weather changes. It is early October and the big boys do need a clip desperately. Midi is a hairy monster, as is William. Still as mischievous as ever, he insists on rearranging his feed bucket in the morning by standing on it.

Tuesday, 6 October

Rats are causing problems again and have been partying on my saddlecloths. They have been eating the nice hayseed bits while sitting on it and then pooing, do they have no shame or what? Paul has put stuff down for them as they have started to go into the house again. They have been coming up through Ben's floor and there are huge holes where they have shoved the bricks on the floor up, hope I don't meet them in the dark.

Here come the vet's best customers again – Eric came in from the field today with a huge cut. It looked as if he had stopped suddenly and somebody had run into the back of him. I was working late and Ann got the vet out. She had to take him to the vet's and he got an ultrasound on his leg and all sorts of other things and had to stay in overnight. Sarah went with them. Apparently Sarah and the vet put their arms round the back of him and shoved him in the trailer. He wouldn't have managed to go in the lorry. He was desperate to come home and all I had to do was give him a little shove on the bum and he went in. Boy, did he stomp until we moved off. The others came whizzing over when they saw us returning. I think William missed him. I put William's night rug on for the first time as it has been cold. He looked as if he felt very special and like a proper horse.

When I work late I ride Ben in the morning and have a lovely hack down the road and a canter up and down the track. He has been going really well but is still skittish.

Ann is finding it hard to get her nerve fully back after her nasty accident. She has been jumping Teddy but keeps having pathetic stops. The only way over it is to keep jumping. Dave came and helped us move the rest of the jumps to the front of the field so we have a good selection with one or two XC types, which is good. We have entered the OTECC at Warwick on Sunday 11, so fingers crossed. We have a jumping lesson on Thursday before we go.

Wednesday, 7 October

Ann drove the lorry to Tesco's to get diesel and only bumped one kerb – I wasn't too traumatised! Like everything else, it is just practice. Got another bit for the gas cooker in the lorry and still can't get it to work. Will need to find someone to do it for us. I only want to be able to make a cup of tea!

Midi has still got a swollen tendon so is inside again. She is like Eric, happy as long as she's eating, so is OK. William is a bit fraught and shouting at her, all his mates are in, bless him. He has to go with the big boys now.

Ben and Teddy are both rather laid back at the moment so we are going to get some competition mix and just give them a handful each. We need a bit of buzz!

Thursday, 8 October

Had our lesson and Ben started off brilliantly. The teacher then put up a brush fence and a parallel with a brush. Ben stopped at the parallel and things only got worse. We both ended up riding with our reins on our nosebands to stop us banging the horses in their mouths. They both went really well, which is bizarre and makes me think perhaps we are both too heavy handed when jumping.

Sunday, 11 October

The weekend went from bad to worse after I lost the earring that OH bought me in Barbados. Ann was, as usual, at the yard up until the last minute. I went to start the lorry and it didn't want to know. It had run out of loopy juice so I promised it one more shot after filling the bit up and it started – phew! Off we went in the fog, Ann asked if I had my lights on – er, yes – er, no, just the fog light, duh! Ann had the directions and off we went and ended up in Leamington Spa! We found the college but the wrong bit, obviously the postcode on the internet was for the college where we were. Ann went in to ask at a hotel and I phoned a friend who works there. We found out that we had a few bridges to go under and no way was I going under them unless I knew the exact height of the lorry, so I got the measuring tape that we luckily had in Ann's handbag (don't ask) and stood at the door of the living, held it up and measured it.

Happy with that, off we went again and eventually found it. I don't know how as we could hardly see in front of us. Anyway, once we got there the fog lifted and it was a lovely day. Mind you, we got there and there were no signs for parking so we opted for a car park with hardstanding.

Started to tack up and oops, no boots for Ben so put the XC ones on. Went to put on my stock and oops, Ann didn't have it, I must have put it somewhere safe. Then I left the lights on and someone came and told me. Got on but while warming up I couldn't get Ben right. I was focused and we went in and went well until the fifth, but he then went a bit scatty and came to the eleventh and he just wasn't looking at the jump so refused twice. I got him over it but was still upset and missed out the fourteenth. I was really, really peed off and swore on the way out.

Ann went in with her hackamore really loose as she only needed steering and not brakes. I could see the tut-tutting from onlookers but he went well and got third. They have now qualified for the final on 23 November at Arena UK. At least the day wasn't wasted. We got back to the lorry and I had forgotten to put the water in. Mind you, the way that I was feeling I could have chucked cold water over Ben. Ann told me I was wicked. We had to negotiate a small opening out of the car park and through a barrier which was up so I had to reverse and squidge out, going over the kerb a bit – said, 'Sorry, Teddy' but said nothing to Ben as I still had a face on with him. I really feel like giving up on the riding and am seriously thinking about having a lesson on one of the jumping schoolmasters just to see if I *can* ride!

Monday, 12 October

Found my lost earring in my purse, don't know how it got there!

Eric has been allowed to go out again after many visits from the vet. He now has a bit of a hang-up about his leg being touched. If you tie him up or try and grab his nose he goes mad. We got round it by having me hold his head-collar rope and talking to him and leaning down while putting the bandage on. He can cope with that and watches me do it. I can then put a boot on.

Thursday, 15 October

Have to take my car to the garage as it keeps doing weird things. I dip my lights and the radio turns down! Got in today and it was lifeless, so got out, locked it, unlocked it and then it was OK. Hmm. Got it booked into the garage for Monday. The weather has suddenly got colder so thicker rugs are in order for outdoors.

Monday, 19 October

Got car sorted, just a problem wire.

William has started to tip his water bucket every day. Don't know why but it has become a habit. Tried putting the bucket in a tyre but he still chucked it everywhere. Then Paul gave me a 56 lb weight to weigh it down and guess what – it worked!

The lorry passed its MOT but had to have the bearings done on the front driver's side. They were absolutely shot to bits, big oops!

Saturday, 24 October

I have got to watch when putting Eric and Will out together because they sometimes rush at the gate if something startles them. Well, they only went and pulled me both ways again today, and not one to let go in case Will won't be caught, I ended up face down in the mud, still hanging on. Big oops!

I know if there are rats about as Will digs at his bed near Teddy's door where they come through. I think he is trying to get them with his hoof. He still has to touch everything with his hoof, I would have thought he would have touched everything with his mouth but this *is* William we are talking about.

November

Was ill for two weeks so not really any riding.

Thursday, 12 November

Ann took Teddy for a lesson before the OTECC final at Arena UK. It was bitterly cold and I had a thermal vest, leggings, jods, two pairs of socks, boots, a polo neck, body warmer, a fleece windproof jacket and a heavy waterproof jacket on, oh, and a woolly hat and gloves. My feet were cold, mind you.

Saturday, 14 November

Ann got clear but wasn't fast enough. It was nearly all kids so I emailed the organisers afterwards and asked if they could have an adult-only class as the horses can't turn as quickly as the ponies. They thanked me for my input.

Sunday, 15 November

Took Ben and Teddy to dressage, it was windy and cold outside but the dressage was inside. Was Ben horrified or what? He kept looking at everything, especially David who was videoing, when we passed him. He went beautifully in the warm-up so I was pleased with him anyway. He just had a little bit of stage fright. I was very calm. Ann's nerves got the better of her, Teddy went really well though. Ah well, next time.

Took William and Midi to the little school on the bypass. Will was a superstar. He went into it no problem and rode round. He even trotted with me on him and went over some poles. Every so often he would see something and stop but then he would go on and he wasn't fazed at all. He wasn't too keen on going into the lorry with the light on as it was dark outside so we loaded Midi on first and then on he went. Charlotte had had great fun on Midi and rode round on her own until Midi got fed up after William stopped and Ann had to shoo her. Then she had two canters with Ann running round. Charlotte was really tired afterwards as I presume Will and Midi were too.

I got on William from the ground for the first time, he looked sort of odd but just stood there. Not bad for a three-year-old.

Monday, 23 November

When we came out of the yard onto the busy bypass I could hear a clunk-clunk. Oh no! We stopped and there was a big lump of limestone brick thingy stuck between the two back tyres. I did what any self-respecting wife would do and phoned OH. He came out with his orange flashlight and chipped away at it with a hammer. He didn't think he could get the last bit so I phoned our mechanic who said not to try and bang it out as the tyre could explode. Arghhh! I shouted at OH to stop and he said he had got most of it. There is a bit still stuck between the metal rims. Too much stress for a Monday evening!

Wednesday, 25 November

Midi has been a little cow-bag and keeps deciding to escape from the field and always takes the babies with her. She legged it towards the next village one day and was caught before she got to the end of the road. Another day the hunt came and set all the horses off. Midi jumped the fence, followed by Eric. William got out too but went to the stables looking for them. Apparently Midi went at a flat-out gallop all the way along the road, up the main road towards the next village and over a ploughed field, hotly pursued by Eric. The huntspeople helped Sarah to catch them and bring them back along the main road. Eric didn't bat an eyelid at the big lorries and the traffic on the way back.

Friday, 27 November

The lorry has been a pain to start so ended up getting two new batteries. I was fed up getting underneath it with the jump leads.

Monday, 30 November

Been going to an indoor school with Sarah and Charlotte, with me on Wills. He is going well but having the odd buck now and then. Charlotte and Midi are doing great and she is cantering herself now.

William is practising weightlifting as he is tipping his water again even with the 56 lb weight in it.

William still runs everywhere in the field, I liken him to a toddler rushing here and there. Eric and Will play and play and play, Eric sometimes even sits down and plays. Sarah and Ann have both seen him do it. Who said we have normal horses?

December

Thursday, 3 December

Had a bit of a shock at work as I was told that I had to drop my hours as business wasn't too good. At first I thought it would be great as I would have more time with our mob but then the thought of losing the money prompted me to search for another job. I sent my CV off to apply for a new position that was being created, went for an interview in Asda's café and got the job. The only problem is that it is full time, which I don't want but I managed to negotiate working from 7 a.m. to 3 p.m. and just have to work out what I will do with the horses.

Tuesday, 29 December

Ann said she will do the horses in the morning so I have accepted the new job.

Christmas has come and gone and we have just tried to keep them all ticking over, time and daylight being the main factor. Nothing significant has happened over these depressing months so haven't written anything. We have booked a holiday to Barbados though and can't wait!

January

Tuesday, 6 January

Started my new job and have to travel thirty-five minutes to get there. This is also the first time ever that I have not gone to the horses first thing in the morning. It is really, really strange! I text Ann I don't know how many times to see if they are OK. Well, all us horsey mums know that only *we* can do our horses correctly! The new job is OK and I can always have a nice horsey chat with my new Aussie mate who used to farm and whose daughters had ponies. He makes me laugh as he always says he 'can't stand the bleeders'.

I am finding fitting the riding in difficult but will persevere.

April

Monday, 7 April

Went on holiday to Barbados over Easter and left the boys with Ann and Sarah. Left my car in the garage as the electrics have been playing up again.

Came back a bit heavier (big oops) and decided to ride Will in the bit of the field we have cornered off. He bucked and bucked most of the way round, how I stayed on I don't know. I ended up pulling the bit through his mouth and stopped him with the rein in his mouth. Got off a bit shaken but made up a round pen, shooed him round and sent him away from me in it the next day. He joined up great and I was really pleased and got on him. I had put another bit in his mouth and strapped his gob shut and he threw a strop. He was tossing his head and throwing himself about and went to go through the fencing. I made him walk round a few times and then got off. I then stuck a big 'for sale' sign on his head and made enquiries about selling him. I don't do dangerous any more.

Thursday, 17 April

I have been lungeing him for about ten days now and he seems to be really accepting the work. He has even popped 2'6" on the lunge and seems to like the jumping bit. I have been on him while on the lunge but am trying to lose a bit of weight first. He measures at about 14.1 hh. now. He has been well behaved and I have given him a reprieve, but if he does the naughty bit again then he is definitely off.

Saturday, 19 April

Ann and I went to pull his mane and I had my back protector and hat on. We twitched him and he was trying to get me by shoving me and tossing me aside with his head. I took my hat and protector off and then he was fine. We reckon somebody has done something to him, possibly tried to back him, with the kit on. Sarah wanted to sell Bailey and I thought about buying him. She has, however, changed her mind since, so we are back to square one.

Sunday, 20 April

William hasn't been shouting at Midi when she is being ridden and he is on his own in the stable, I guess he is growing up a bit more now because he is working.

Paul has ploughed the fields we use for exercising so we have to move to the back paddock. It will have to be sorted out first which is a pain. I did say to Sarah that if there is nowhere to exercise then I will be moving as there is no way I am going out on the road with Will. Ben is bad enough, the other day we came across a killer field roller which was hidden in the corner of a field as we rode out. We spun round, went backwards, nearly ended up in the ditch… need I say any more? I got off him, led him up to it, then took him away, then back and got on him. He was wary at first but then went OK. The next day I rode up to the hill and passed a magpie caught in a cage, Ben was hysterical at the sight of that as well but I got him past it. He managed to go himself on the way home though as he knew that was the way out of the field. Oh, for a nice quiet ride!

Tuesday, 29 April

The yard is absolutely minging because of the sheep, there's mud all over my car. It needs a new alternator as it is doing funny things with the electrics. Is it me or are there lots of odd cars around?

Teddy was going really well and Ann was having jumping lessons. She put a hackamore on him and he was jumping fine. Then he started to take the p★★s and started to refuse jumps. She got him a tens machine for his back and has ordered a new saddle which is being specially made for him. We went to two one-day events and he was eliminated both times at the first jump. We braved the howling winds at the first one and he just wouldn't jump when he got in the ring. Same at Eland Lodge, he wasn't interested. I have managed to sort Ann's riding out since I came back though and Teddy's flat work is great. She has been using a contraption to keep his head in as well as to help build up his muscles. This is all great but he still doesn't want to jump. I suggested she put the baby bit in and jump him in it. He is getting better, so fingers crossed.

Wednesday, 30 April

Eric has been lunged and got confused about both reins but he is getting there. Ann's thinking is that she had better start doing him now before he gets bigger and stronger. Mind you, he is about 16.1 hh. at the moment. He is still in your face a bit, but is getting there.

The show season is kicking off again so we might do a bit of in-hand with the babies and take Charlotte along with Midi.

William jumping with a 'for sale' sign on his head.

May

Friday, 2 May

I have been riding William in the back field and he has been putting in the occasional buck when I have tried to canter him. He has had me off twice, which made me throw a temper tantrum and call him all sorts of names.

Saturday, 3 May

After all the shenanigans of bucking and throwing paddies, William was put on the horsemart website for £1,400 o.n.o. Put a cracking photo of him jumping 3 ft on the lunge and I had loads of enquiries, but were they time-wasters or what? Had one girl come and have a look at him and she didn't go near him, she just patted him a bit. She didn't even come with her joddies on and she thought that he was further on in his training than he was. She was based near us and I was willing to put him on loan to the right person if need be. Someone else was supposed to phone me back and arrange to come but she didn't. Loads of people phoned and asked stupid questions. I ended up writing on the web that his price reflected his experience. It was only £1,400 o.n.o! Lots of people asked if he hacked out, er, no, he is a baby! Now since he has had a 'for sale' sticker on his head he has behaved. I had someone phone after four weeks and said that they thought he was really underpriced as he has done a lot more work under the saddle than you would expect for £1,400.

Tuesday, 6 May

A lady phoned who teaches 'natural horsemanship' and wanted the tack included and the price dropped. I definitely don't think so! I said that his price reflected his experience i.e. he's not done much, but that he has had *some* training.

Will's flat work is coming on nicely. I have been lungeing him before riding him and he is doing a lot of canter work now and managing not to lean on the lunge line. He has a lovely pop and does 3 ft with ease. When he gets going forward I think he will be really good. He can do a half-decent circle when ridden and walks with his head down. You can pick him up slightly to make his walk a bit more collected. He can trot with his head in as well. His only vice is his buck when he gets a bit fed up. He decked me after stopping, bucking and dropping his shoulder, a typical pony. I feel like the resident stunt rider!

Thursday, 8 May

Had bad news about my Aussie mate who has terminal cancer, it made me really think; that we are not invincible and how I want to compete now. The plan was to bring on and eventually compete William but not wishing to appear like a spoilt brat, I don't want to wait, I want to do it now!

I have decided that Ben has had enough of competing, I didn't realise how bad his paces were. I had a jumping lesson on him and he was just rushing and diving over everything, which was not at all enjoyable. The plan was to get something else to compete with, as he is feeling his aches and pains now and not jumping well at all and I am not getting any younger either. I think he should semi-retire now and am looking for someone to keep him ticking over. Have started looking but nothing seems to smack me in the face.

Saturday, 10 May

Our farrier was selling a chestnut mare so we popped up to see her. As soon as I saw her I thought that she was lovely but just not right. She jumped like Teddy and when you got on her you had to stay off her back or she would walk off straight away. I thought that was all a bit dodgy but rode her anyway. She was very strong and had to be bullied down on the bit. I declined to jump her because I like to be in control. There were quite a few things about her that I didn't think were right, but went home to think about it.

I decided not to buy her because I just don't have the extra time to retrain her like she needs. While Sarah went on holiday for a few days I was riding Bailey – it meant I could gauge how much time I would have to ride if I had another. Not much it turns out, if you have to school two. I probably will keep Will as he is going well, however, I have told him not to unpack his suitcase just yet because if he is naughty he goes! He was a bit funny in the field and wouldn't be caught for a while but seems to have settled again. I have left his head collar on so it is easier. He is such a complicated little person.

I decided to ask a friend if she would like to come and keep Ben ticking along as he is not ready yet to retire completely. She said she will come when she can.

The car's electrics are still playing up, the door lock sometimes works and sometimes doesn't. It has been in that many times I have been told they are going to get a chair with my name on it! It does get washed and cleaned when it is in though, which is great as I don't have time to do it.

Sunday, 11 May

My friend came and tried Ben and I popped on him and did ride and lead with Will. He was confused but got the idea, only in walk though. Ann was lungeing Charlotte on Midi and I rode Will round with my friend who was riding Ben, then trotted up the hill on him on my own. The ground in the little back paddock is awful, with loads of holes which have been dug by someone who was looking for buried metal objects with his metal detector. The only thing is that he doesn't fill in the holes he makes afterwards!

Tuesday, 13 May

Midi has sweet itch and likes to scratch her huge rear end on the gate and the wall in her stable. She decided to do this one evening at about 12.30 and in the house they all heard an almighty crash. Sarah and Paul came rushing out to see Midi stuck to the far wall of her stable, horrified, Will stuck the far end of his stable, horrified, and the gate into Midi's stable lying on the ground. In her enthusiasm while scratching, the gate had lifted off and toppled onto the floor.

William was also scratching against the short bit of wall in his stable, which is made of breeze blocks. They were not put up properly and while he was scratching his chunky bum he loosened the wall and the blocks were hanging precariously the next morning. I think their tails all need a good wash and comb. I suppose if you have an itch you gotta scratch it!

Wednesday, 14 May

Midi has a lovely pink muzzle to wear so she can go out in the field. Funnily enough she doesn't get wheezy when she wears it and is looking good and much slimmer. She managed to get it off twice but seems to have settled down with it now. Bailey could do with one as well. Sarah said if I get another horse she will put Bailey in the barn. The only thing is where will Bailey go as the indoor school is planned for where Bailey's makeshift stable will be?

Sarah and I went to the horse sales in town. I promised to keep my hands in my pockets when we went to watch the bidding. There were some nice horses there. We also saw a friend who told us her son is giving up competing, etc. and going to go travelling. She had brought two horses to the market and said they had twenty to sell!

Saturday, 17 May

Went to look at a lovely Danish warmblood gelding near Corby, Northants. He was really nice and seemed friendly. The owner said that because he is only six he can be a bit naughty sometimes (a bit like Will) anyway, she was riding him but only went round the edge of the school. I asked to see him canter and he then threw a bit of a paddy, not much, but a paddy nonetheless. I got on him and rode him in circles and across the school and he was a dream to ride. I asked for canter and got some strides and then he threw a strop. He bucked, tossed his head, bucked again, reared, then reared even higher. I pushed him on and changed the rein and he did the same on the other rein. Is he a spoilt brat or what? Ann was videoing and Sarah was watching. I said I would let my husband watch the video before I made a decision. OH watched just enough to see him bucking and rearing and then refused to watch any more. 'Hmm,' I said, 'I suppose that is a no then!' Poor Sarah needed a fag as soon as we got home. So no chestnut mares and no Danish warmbloods! Funnily enough we had just been talking about warmbloods the day before and saying how funny they can be.

Monday, 19 May

Now this made me feel a bit dejected; travelling all that way and the horses turning out to be a bit loopy, so I phoned the chap who was selling his horses locally and asked him what he had for sale. He had some mares so we popped up to see them. (He is only at the bottom of our road.) One grey mare came over to us and put her chin on my arm. I felt that I had been picked! I agreed to come back on the Friday and try her. She went really nicely and has a huge pop. I got on her and had a bit of difficulty in getting her going. The saddle was really uncomfortable and I ride differently to showjumpers. (She is a grade C showjumper.) OH and Sarah came with me as Ann was poorly. It was raining and not a nice day at all. They both liked her and OH suggested I buy her. I waited until Saturday to text him and then the deal was done.

Saturday, 24 May

Told Will and Ben and Ben had a face on. When I went into the stable he went over to Teddy and put his head over the door. Oops, what a bad mother I am! Will has been going really well but with all the hoo-ha of looking for another horse I have left him for a few days and haven't done much.

Thursday, 29 May

We picked the new horse up this evening and took Midi along with us so she would have someone to talk to on the way home. Her owner said she sort of jumps onto the ramp and then into the lorry. She didn't want to go in first so we put Midi in and then put her on the back. She got up the ramp but couldn't figure out how to turn round to stand sideways.

Lesson: If you get a new horse it is a good idea to take one which will be with it in the field to collect it, this gives them the chance to meet and bond a bit before they are turned out. Tying up two horses that need to get on lets them get to know one another as well.

Friday, 30 May

Bailey has moved across to the big shed and Eric is beside Teddy with the new horse at the end. I decided that I didn't like her name so have called her Lucy. Her front shoe got pulled off in the mud and could I get the farrier to come? No. He said he would try and get someone he knew near us to come instead but I heard nothing all weekend. She was booked to go to the vet on Wednesday but will have to put that off and leave her until the following Friday, when the farrier can come down. I am pig-sick. I think we might have to think about getting a farrier nearer to home.

I rescheduled the vetting and changed my day off work – argh, I don't need this hassle. You don't realise how important your farrier actually is until you need them. The old saying, 'No foot, no horse' really is true because if your horse's shoe comes off you are stuffed!

Lesson: Look after your farrier, he really is a very, very important person in your life!

Saturday, 31 May

Rode Lucy in the field with one shoe missing and she went OK, on the second day I even had a small pop on her which was just… wow! Of course this loosened the two back shoes which are now hanging on by a thread. Don't you just love horses!

June

Monday, 2 June

I have been doing some work on the ground with Lucy and she doesn't seem to be the sharpest tool in the box but is sweet and seems to have settled in easily. She is out with Midi in a fenced-off bit of the field and those girls just don't stop eating!

Wednesday, 4 June

William is in love with Lucy and kept barging through the leccy fence, so we had to electrify it. He knows what it does now and so does Eric as they both got too near it the other day and it zapped, which made them all run off.

As the girls are in one field and boys in the other, I bring the girls in then go for the boys, just shout and *woosh*, they coming whizzing over, usually Will first. They seem to know that Bailey comes in first, then the girl then the rest of them, it certainly makes life a bit easier. The big boys can be rude sometimes and ignore you and you have to walk all the way to the furthest point of the field to get them.

Friday, 6 June

Changed Will's bit for a snaffle with cheek pieces. He seems to like it and doesn't try and get his tongue over the bit. It is also easier to steer him with it on.

Charlotte has been riding Midi round off the lunge in the paddock. We have fenced off a bit and she quite happily trots round, kicking Midi and trying to canter.

Me training up William.

Saturday, 7 June

Been lungeing Will before riding him and have got him cantering more and more; he gets cheeky and bucks a bit but is getting the hang of it. He goes by voice commands; walk, trot and 'tup' for canter. If you put your hand up he stops and comes over to it for a fuss. I have been having little canters while riding him and bless, he has been good, only for little short bursts mind you, but he is starting to understand what I mean. I also had a little jump on him and he was so taken by surprise that he leapt about three feet in the air! The second time he just trotted over it. He doesn't seem to be bothered about actually jumping small fences, he just trots over them.

Am cantering Will a bit more and he isn't doing too badly, he isn't going forward as much in canter as he does in trot, but he is getting there. If you put your hand on his withers he stops, this seems to be his brake switch although you do have to be careful when he stops suddenly lest you go out the front door.

Sunday, 8 June

Went to an ODE with Teddy and Sarah came with Bailey to do the XC. She decided she didn't want to do it and so I took him round. I knew that if I got him to the fences he would jump them. We went sideways quite a bit and backed off from a few strange things but I got him round and had a fantastic time. I am glad I did it because before I rode him round I had been getting very despondent and fed up and wondered why I had horses at all.

Took Ben into the field and rode him with Charlotte on Midi. She wanted to canter so I cantered Ben round and she followed. Her little legs and arms were going everywhere and she was shouting 'Look, Mummy' at Ann, who was lungeing Eric. She reminds me of those little Thelwell ponies. I dread to think what would happen if Midi suddenly went sideways or stopped. Ben took his duties really seriously and didn't grump once at Midi.

Saturday, 14 June

Been riding Lucy but I don't feel happy, she feels too big for me and when I jumped her she scared the s★★t out of me as she jumped so high. My confidence seems to be at rock-bottom when riding at the moment and I am thinking about letting Ann ride her. Am totally confused and disappointed but won't make any hasty decisions.

Friday, 20 June

Ann has gone on holiday for a week so I am doing six horses. Had to take half days at work because it is just too much to do in my spare time. Been trying to ride whoever I can. Lucy had her teeth done and isn't getting ridden for a week so I am lungeing her. Got on Will bareback and rode him up to the paddock and round it twice, had a little trot and brought him back down, he was a star.

Saturday, 21 June

Got Sarah to ride Ben and then got David to come and ride Ben as well. Rode Teddy in Will's bit and he seemed to find it OK. Teddy is getting annoyed by his hay fever again and sometimes snatches his head up. I have started putting Vaseline on everyone's feet again and they are all looking good for it. I asked the big boys if they would be kind enough to come when I call because I am very tired and bless them they have been coming as well.

Tuesday, 24 June

I have been having to put them out at 5.30 a.m. so I can go home to get changed and get to work for 7 a.m. Horses are not for the faint-hearted! By the time I bring them in they are all fat, with big wobbly bellies, I couldn't leave them out all the time. Mind you, I don't think they would stay out anyway, at the first sign of flies they are at the gate.

Wednesday, 25 June

I managed to bring all four boys in at once, which was a miracle. You just have to shove them a bit and then tell them where to move to and to behave. I tell them that I am only little so they have to be good.

Lucy is being a poppet when handled but is sometimes a bit funny with her back legs being picked up. If she tries to kick me she gets a slap and I get a funny look off her in return, but it seems to be working.

Thursday, 26 June

Will seems to be happy to be worked and when he is he has a nice tidy bed the next morning. He was digging holes in his bed again but I think it is because he can hear the bees in the wall and maybe sniff the honey. He only seems to do it if there are mice, rats or something else nearby. He has stopped tipping his water bucket. I bought him a sturdy plastic one which obviously isn't as much fun to chuck around and doesn't tip easily.

Friday, 27 June

The groundwork with Lucy has helped me to bond with her, which is good and I have even started to ride her. I had a lovely ride one day and have decided that I will ride and compete her but still go for lessons.

Will is trotting round nicely and can circle not too badly. I continue to pop him over poles on the lunge and small ones on his back. He doesn't respect small jumps though and just trots up to them and over. If there is a pole on the ground it sometimes horrifies him and he trots up, stops, goes forward, stops, goes back, forward, back, forward, snorts and then goes over it. I can't help but laugh.

Saturday, 28 June

I have been practising backward and sideward movements while doing groundwork with Will as I would like to dance with him... to music... er, well, it is just something I want to do so I am going to work at it... Watch this space!

Car's electrics are still going doolally, the new lock parts work well but the radio keeps turning itself down and going off. Also, I really don't think it was -40° outside in June, not even in England!

Me riding Lucy in the paddock before the fall out.

July

Thursday, 3 July

Started my lessons and Lucy has had her noseband tightened right up and I have to be really forceful with her. She is funny going into the lorry, you have to shoo her in and she sort of canters in and turns her bum round. The whole lorry shakes. She is a bit of a pain to mount and we have to spend time at the mounting block to get her to stand beside it, she moves, I shoo her back, she moves…

Friday, 4 July

Will seems quite happy doing cross poles with me on him so I decided to put him at a 2'3" upright, which he popped nicely. He then cantered off nearly all the way round the school, which was good. He still has a bit of a grump if you ask for a canter with leg and he still likes you to say 'tup' which he knows from the lunge. He sort of bucks when he has cantered enough but is not nasty with it.

Sunday, 6 July

Charlotte asked if we could ride down the road bareback, *Great idea*, I thought and popped on William, who started bucking across the yard and promptly dumped me in the most horrible, mucky puddle you can imagine. I was absolutely filthy. I think when I got on him I must have kicked him or something. I had to de-gunge myself in the cold water and of course buy a new hat as my head had hit the hard floor.

> *Lesson*: never ever get complacent with horses they are a great at putting you in your place when you think everything is OK and you know it all.

Monday, 7 July

I think the fall off William affected me a bit as I had to go to the doctor's. He just looked at me when I said my legs wouldn't work properly. Well, they wouldn't! It felt like an effort to move them and I had difficulty getting on Will from the ground. One anti-inflammatory tablet later and I started to feel a whole lot better, thank goodness.

The field was topped and you can see the jumps now, which made William see a monster at the gate! We put the water tray out between two barrels and got Will to follow Midi past it. He skipped to the side of it and as the gap got smaller he actually tiptoed over it. Ann then put a pole on top of the barrels, which were on their side, and he popped it first time. What a superstar, he is definitely going to be a jumper. Midi likes to trot behind him but as he is forward going that is not a problem.

Saturday, 12 July

Have been practising getting on at the bench we have for mounting. I had to move it out at first so that Will was sandwiched between the wall and the mounting bit. After about five goes he let me get on by just walking up to it normally. I put boots on his front legs and he made me laugh; he stomped out of his stable lifting his legs up but he did look proud! They were a bit big so will have to buy some others for him. I have started to wash his face after exercise as well as his sweaty bits to get him used to it. He still yawns his head off when he has been exercised. He is still coming to call with Eric and being caught no problem, although he still has his head collar on in the field.

Sunday, 13 July

Paul said that Lucy and Will have been playing up and down the electric fence, which is good. Have been having 'beastings' in my lessons, which I call my aerobic workout and Lucy is coming on fine, although she has a rub on her face from either the bit or the noseband. I have jumped her and she is so different from Will. He just dinks over the fence she just goes like... wow! She is still having problems picking off on her right-leg canter so am working on that with a pole on the ground.

Thursday, 17 July

Will still likes to stop at puddles and have a look and a splash, it should be interesting when he goes to a water jump. I would like to take him to the cross-country course before the end of the season, just to jump some small ones and to canter round and go in the water.

Friday, 18 July

Lucy double-barrelled Teddy in the field after we had ridden the other day, the horses were standing still and we were all talking and for no reason she just backed up to him and kicked him. I told Ann to get the vet out, just to check him over. He is fine but grumps every time he sees Lucy. (Yet another vet's bill.)

Thursday, 24 July

I am trying to perfect Will's actions so that I can hopefully take him to do a dressage test. Time is the problem as Lucy needs more work than I thought. Ben is still being ridden by my friend and has even had a little pop over a jump. He seems happy and doesn't nark at Will when he is tied up outside his stable, he just eats Will's hay.

Saturday, 26 July

If Will was for sale now you could say that he is going forward nicely, sometimes working on the bit. He is cantering and jumping small jumps and can do a few in a row. He can be caught, is nice to handle and tack up and can be mounted from a mounting block. He loads OK as well.

He still mugs his feed bucket and turns it upside down and he is still playing with his ball. In the morning after he has eaten he puts both feet in his bucket and just stands there. If you go in to pick a poo up and don't shut his door properly he legs it outside for a look but you can chase him in because he knows he is being cheeky and isn't frightened. He doesn't really like the seaweed in his dinner and will leave it if you put too much in it. How on earth can he eat all the food except for the seaweed granules?

The car is still being odd, I suppose it should go back in because it does need a wash!

August

Saturday, 2 August

We are able to use the fields on the hill for the moment and have been taking the big boys up there. My plan is to take Will and try and get a long canter with him. Should be interesting in the open field.

Sunday, 3 August

Took Lucy into the big field and she was fine, I am still hanging onto her a bit but I even managed a canter round with Teddy when we went up on our own the next day and she matched his lovely long stride.

Tuesday, 5 August

Still going for lessons and Lucy is boxing really well and goes straight on. I wear my hat when tacking her up in the lorry as I have bashed my head twice and got squashed against the partition. You live and learn. I am trying to teach her to get ready in the lorry because I don't trust her to be tied up outside with another horse, since she double-barrelled Teddy.

> *Lesson*: always wear the correct PPE (Personal Protective Equipment) when handling a new horse.

Wednesday, 6 August

Eric and Will are still as thick as thieves and play together just as often. Ann has been lungeing Eric and he has a face on if he doesn't get to do any work. She has also sat on him although he did rush forwards with a confused look on his face when she did. The idea is to stop any problems before they start. My experiences with Will have prepared us for all this.

Took Teddy and Lucy XC training. She and Teddy travelled

fine together in the lorry although he wouldn't look at her and stared at the back door all the way there. We got Teddy ready outside the lorry and Lucy ready inside it. She didn't bat an eyelid when I got her off and even let me get on at the lorry step. I was hanging onto her a lot going round the course and was very worried, we ran out at a few jumps but she jumped ditches, up and down ones and some big ones. It was fun and we had a gallop up the hill. I think we will do better when I stop hanging onto her; she gets confused. Definitely going again!

Thursday, 7 August

Locked my keys in the lorry and could we break in? Oh no, not even through the back. I had to get a bit of wire and go in through the door – children, please do not try this at home. I felt a right plonker, Ann is going to get a second set of keys made.

Went for a short walk down the road with Will, Teddy and Ben; Will was quite happy and forward going. He stopped for a play in a puddle on the way out, he still likes to splash.

Sunday, 10 August

I have changed Will's work a bit now and he is doing leg yields. He has taken to it quite well but if you go right he will keep going and going until you give him a sharp kick to go the other way. He has done a really nice attempt at a turn on the forehand although he does have difficulty standing still. His back legs were really coming under him and he was starting to show some elevation in his paces. There is hope for him yet. While asking for a leg yield he started to do a canter pirouette so I thought, *Hey why not?* and he now does a very good attempt both ways. Way to go, Will!

The next day I did lots of exercises again and was put in my place by Will bucking when I used too much leg for the canter, oops, sorry, Will! I finished off by leading him round, with Charlotte riding to give him a break from my weight. Horses keep you honest, if you get smart they put you in your place. Charlotte put him to bed and hugged and kissed him and told him she loved him. He seems to have accepted her now and can cope when she makes sharp movements.

Sunday, 17 August

Having decided that I would like to dance with William I have also being doing lots of movements sideways, backwards and forwards on the lunge. He really is a sharp little cookie and is getting the hang of it.

Tuesday, 19 August

Went for another lesson with Lucy and while we were away Midi let herself out of the stable and walked across the road to eat the nice grass in the small bit next to our field. I don't think that Charlotte shut the door properly.

The lessons with Lucy have been fine but I feel that the strong tactics we have been using are just not me and so I have decided that I will go for another jumping lesson and then give the rest of the lessons a miss and do it my way. She has come on a bit but it just isn't my style and I am going to train her as if she is a retrain, which I suppose technically she is because she was a showjumper. I hate having a really tight noseband on her and all sorts of bits in her mouth. I have only ever used a noseband for show and I feel as if I am going against my own methods.

Wednesday, 20 August

Rode Lucy after my decision, slackened the noseband a bit and warmed her up and rode her my way. She went lovely and so I jumped her. She went the best she has ever gone and I think I have made the right decision. I feel I have really bonded with her and don't want to bully her into submission. Ben and Will listen to me because they want to and I would like Lucy to do the same.

She is lovely to work in all respects now and has really become one of the family. Being away with Teddy seems to have integrated her into the mob now, even though they are not in the same field. She grooms Midi over her door and was even grooming Eric over his.

Sunday, 24 August

Ben is happily being ridden by my friend and they are still leading Midi round without a grump in sight. We all rode down the road to finish off one day and they all seemed happy enough, though Lucy wasn't too impressed.

Tuesday, 26 August

The car is finally sorted. It needed a whole new wiring loom in the bonnet and it is now working beautifully so I suppose I will now have to wash and clean it myself – drat!

Thursday, 28 August

Sarah's trailer got pinched from the front of the yard. The horses have been a bit funny for a few days so we think someone might have been creeping about. It freaks me out a bit thinking that somebody might be watching us.

September

Saturday, 6 September

Just when you think everything is going well…

I jumped Lucy and came off twice, we went over the jump and I decided to go right; she went one way, I went the other. I knew which way I wanted to go after the jump and altered my weight accordingly but obviously we weren't talking the same language! I am really, really fed up and want to give up horses. Horses are great at bringing you down to earth, you feel wonderful and think all is going well, then whoops, off you come. I think I am a bit down because I had bad news about my old boss's son, who died in a car crash. What a waste, it makes you think.

Monday, 8 September

Back to the doctors as my legs won't work properly again!

Thursday, 11 September

Took Lucy for a saddle fitting and he said she wasn't looking right on one side and he wouldn't sell me a saddle until I had her checked. Booked the massage lady who seemed to sort her out a bit and made her more supple. If I had had a massage like she did I would be supple as well!

Friday, 12 September

Rode William who always cheers me up.

Decided that coming off Lucy is not what I want so I booked a riding clinic for a week and will make the decision whether to keep her or not after that. Loaded her in the lorry with all my belongings and off I went on my own to the Cotswolds. I was driving down the M69 thinking, *What on earth am I doing?*

Monday, 15 September

Got there, settled Lucy and met another girl who was staying at the same B&B. She offered to take me and my case down to the B&B as I didn't fancy walking. Lucy was really well behaved the whole time. I had told her that she was going on holiday so when she got in her stable she just wanted to stay in all the time and eat! I went to get her out and she went to the corner and tried to hide, 'Er, hello,' I said, 'I know you are on holiday but you have to work!'

Trying to ride a different way was quite difficult as it is completely unlike how I have been riding all these years. I had jumping lessons in the afternoons and I think that I wasn't riding correctly. As the week went on I went on a complete downer and came off while jumping on the Thursday. I didn't ride into the fence, she stopped, I got dumped, got up, burst into tears and wanted to just put her into the box and go home. Apart from all the upset it was a good week but I decided to sell her anyway as I was really fed up; she makes me feel like I can't ride. I am so upset, I bought this lovely natured horse who has so much talent and is well, just gorgeous, and I can't ride her! Mind you, I have always felt small on her. But then Teddy is the same size, if not bigger and I don't feel small on him.

Friday, 19 September

Came home from my 'holiday' and Ann asked if she could take Lucy for a jumping lesson. She did and got on really well, she loves riding her and said that she wanted to buy her from me. She will have to sell Eric though if she does want to buy her. I started to ride Teddy and she has taken on Lucy.

William, bless him, is really good even when he isn't ridden for a few days then I can get on him again. We took him into the big front field and I gave him quite a long canter and off he went, he didn't want to trot, he was off!

Saturday, 20 September

Sarah, Ann and I went to Brooksby to do the OTECC challenge. I had only been riding Teddy for about a week and didn't feel happy, I felt as if I couldn't ride him as well. Anyway, off we went, I rode like a bag of s★★t. I came out feeling as if I still couldn't ride and really, really wanted to give horses up, until we had the results: I got second and Ann got third on Lucy! Sarah was too slow to be placed but got round. That cheered me up a bit and we both qualified for the final on 4 December at Arena UK. Can't wait till next year for Will to do it as I think he will be good at it.

The lorry was funny about starting before we went and the light switch had been left on. I know I checked it, it seems a bit odd.

Wednesday, 24 September

Been riding Teddy in the fields and twice he has gone down on his knees with me on him. It's not good at all and my left leg and hip are now hurting. The ground has got awful and we are now feeling very despondent about the whole place.

Thursday, 25 September

Lucy and Midi got out of the field and were on their way to the next village again! Sarah came down the road and Lucy turned round, Midi followed and Sarah put them in.

Friday, 26 September

Lucy got out over the fence and was walking up the lane, looking over the hedge. Luckily I was there and could see this grey head looking over the hedge. She came when I called and looked a bit bemused and couldn't figure out why she was one side of the fence and Midi the other.

Tuesday, 30 September

Charlotte has suddenly come on in leaps and bounds and is trotting Midi round nicely in the small paddock and doesn't have to kick as much now.

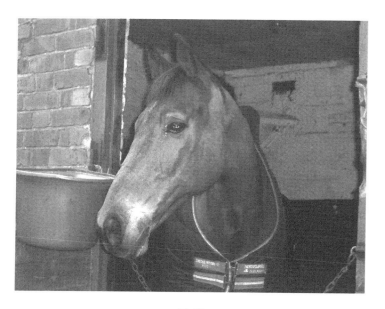

Teddy

October

Friday, 3 October

Tried jumping Teddy on the slippery grass in a hackamore and he seemed to go OK so I will use it for the competition tomorrow.

Saturday, 4 October

The lorry didn't want to start before we went to Moreton Morrell to do the OTECC and had to have a jump from Paul's truck. There was a bit of confusion over where the positive lead was, I said at the front so he put it on the front battery and not at the front where the cab was. Big oops, his battery started smoking in the truck! I sort of coughed and said, 'Ahem, I don't think that should be smoking, should it?' The odd thing was there was a switch on inside the cab, I know that I didn't switch anything on as I don't even know what that switch is for. The driver's door was open as well and I am sure that I didn't unlock it. I think someone has been mooching around. It was parked round the front in what we now call the 'Nick and Park Car Park'.

Drove to OTECC and we only got lost again! I must have turned the lorry round about four times. Ann was reading the directions, same as last year, so I guess it was no surprise. Coming home was a doddle and I now know how to get there!

My blood pressure must have been off the scale by the time we arrived and I got my bossy head on and told Ann and Sarah to get the horses off, get themselves ready and I would go for a wee and get the numbers. I then decided that I was going to remember to breathe, stay calm and enjoy myself. I got eighth on Teddy and Ann got eliminated at a XC fence. Sarah had a stop and a knock down. Teddy really listened to me and it was only the second time that I had jumped him in a hackamore. I really concentrated and used my legs to turn him and he was a superstar. I thought, *I can ride*! I could have done better if I hadn't gone past number ten, it was very close to the one before it and before I knew it, I was there. I couldn't see the number clearly, I think I could do with wearing specs when jumping!

Sunday, 5 October

We are looking for another yard as Ann and I are both very despondent about riding, etc. It was very wet and they all had to stay in. I let Will and Midi out into the small enclosed bit in front of the stables for a pick of the grass. They groomed and then Will went and caused a riot with Lucy and made her squeal. Ann then let Eric out and they played and bit each other and bucked and cantered about in this small space. I then had to put them in because they were too rowdy.

Monday, 6 October

The car said it was -40° this morning – does this mean I might get to put it back into the garage? It could do with a wash!

Wednesday, 8 October

Will doesn't seem to be as scared now if I wear a hat or a coat when it is wet. He gets a bit freaked if it is windy though. He has also started picking up the feed dropped out of his feed bowl with his teeth, he ever so carefully bites the ground to pick the bits off – poor starving pony!

Friday, 10 October

Exercising them at the moment is awful, I daren't ride Teddy in the field in case he trips. We can't ride unless we are both there and there are no more liveries, it is just not safe to ride on your own. We really like it here but it is not practical if we want to ride all winter. Money is going to be the issue if we move.

Saturday, 11 October

William has decided that he doesn't like his feed, I put it in his box and he just looks at me, so I have had to try it without garlic, then without oil, with sugar beet, then with nuts. He seems to prefer his Happy Hoof with a few nuts, a little bit of garlic and just a splosh of sugar beet. Is he spoilt or what?

Sunday, 12 October

I have mentioned to Ann about her buying Lucy again and she said she will sell Eric. The lorry needs painting and I would like to use some of the money for that. I want to spend more time bringing Will on and will help out with Teddy. Lucy and I just don't get on and that is that. Sometimes you just have to admit it.

Monday, 13 October

Took Looby Loo (Lucy) to get a saddle fitted. The one we are using is pinching her and she has gone backwards a bit and is rushing her fences so she needs a fitted one. I always say to the saddle fitter that I don't want an expensive one, but one that fits. He always laughs and asks what is expensive, because some people think £100 is expensive. I usually mutter and say I don't care what colour or make it is, just that it fits. We tried a few and then he brought the last of the bargains out, which luckily fitted and it was half price, big phew! OH says for every £1,000 I spend he should get £100 to go fishing, the saddle was only £350, so that was a bargain. Mind you, the saddle cloth with sheepskin was £63.99 but I figured that since I saved £350...

Sunday, 19 October

Since it was a beautiful sunny day on Sunday we decided the horses should be clipped. Teddy was done first and as usual was a poppet and just stood still. Ann tried to get near Lucy with the clippers and she was having none of it, she pushes you out of the way and since she is such a big girl it can be quite dangerous, so we put Lucy in Midi's stable so that she could see the clipping being done. William was in his stable next to Teddy and could see all the happenings as well.

I can't clip any more as the horsehair makes me really wheezy so Ann has to do it all. Lucy was quite interested in the goings-on so Ann put the clippers over the stable door and clipped a bit of Lucy's neck. She seemed fine with this so Ann went into the stable and clipped her in there. She seems to feel secure if she can have her head over a door.

After Ann had clipped Lucy she went into William's stable and he snorted and backed off, she persevered and managed to clip the front of the neck, argh, I thought, I have a pink pony! Midi was clipped fully out, even her mane and the top of her tail, I then bathed her and washed Teddy's mane, tail and legs. Ben will be done next weekend. Rode Teddy in the field and his leg slipped back, he really can't cope with the slippery grass so I didn't do much. Ann rode Lucy and she was really sweaty so we think she will need to be clipped fully out.

Monday, 20 October

Saw a yard advertised in the local feed merchant's and Ann phoned to see where it was. It is a bit further for us to travel but has a manège and an indoor school is half-built. We went over to have a look and said that we would be bringing six and then possibly selling one so it would be five eventually. She did us a deal and we took Charlotte over for a look and it felt really nice, we have said that we will go at the end of October, just don't know how we are going to tell Sarah.

This is my most favourite picture of Charlotte and Midi, which I just had to include. Look at Charlotte's legs, how she stayed on is a mystery. Thankfully she doesn't have to kick as much now. This picture always cheers me up, now that is someone having fun!

To be continued…

141

Glossary

Affiliated Events   events run by British Eventing which you
                        have to be a member of to compete in.

Aids   use of legs, hands, voice, etc.

Bit   the metal piece which goes into a horse's
                        mouth.

Brush Fence   a brown fence with branches from a tree
                        sticking up to make it look like a brush.

Cricket Score   used when you have lots of poles down when
                        jumping and your points add up i.e. four
                        faults for a pole down.

Coloured   a black-and-white, brown-and-white or
                        grey-and-white horse.

Hanging Snaffle   a type of bit which uses the poll (top of
                        horse's head) action to control it the horse.

Chair   a cross-country jump which looks like a huge
                        long chair.

COPD   a respiratory disease.

Cross Country   where you ride over a course of natural
                        obstacles set over a large distance i.e. two or
                        three fields and/or through woods, water,
                        etc.

Double-barrel Kick   when a horse kicks out with both back legs at
                        once.

Dressage   a competition for both horse and rider to test
                        their suppleness and obedience with a set
                        format in a measured-out arena.

Fillers   things which are put under jumping poles to
                        make the jump look as if is filled in, could
                        look like a wall, or boards painted with
                        flowers, squiggles, etc.

Flat   as in flat work, means not jumping.

Flexion	a test to see how the horse reacts when the leg is held up, usually a test for lameness.
Fly Rug	a mesh rug designed to cover the whole of the horse to keep off flies.
Forehand	a horse is on the forehand when it puts more weight onto the front legs when working.
Gelding	a castrated male horse.
Hackamore	a bit-less bridle, designed to use pressure on the nose rather than the mouth.
Hacking	riding out in the countryside or along the road.
Head Collar	goes on the head and has a rope attached, but does not have a bit to go in the mouth; used for leading and tying up the horse.
Hock	on the horses back leg, a bit like an elbow.
Hogged Mane	a term used when the mane is all shaved off.
In-hand Canter	when the canter is controlled and fairly slow.
Joining Up	when you work with the horse, it accepts you as its leader.
Leg Yield	this is when the horse moves away from your leg to the side.
Lunge	the horse is on a long rope working away from you.
Manège	an arena with a sand or rubber surface for you to work your horse on.
Mucking Out	cleaning out the horse's stable.
Myler	a type of bit that lets each side of the bit move independently.
Numnah	the saddle cloth which is put under a saddle.
Oxer	a type of horse jump with two rails that may be set even or uneven. The width between the poles may vary.
Pairs	usually in cross country where two riders go round a set course together.

144

Parallel Fence	both the top front and back rail are even, but the jump is higher than it is wide.
PPE	Personal Protection Equipment i.e. hard hat, back protector, steel-toe-cap boots and gloves.
Pinging	a term we use when a horse is jumping enthusiastically with a spring in its jump.
Purple Spray	an antiseptic spray used for cuts which is purple and if you get it on your fingers it doesn't wash off for about a week.
Putting Out	taking the horse to the field.
Sending Away	making the horse move away from you out onto a circle.
Schoolmaster	a horse which gives its rider confidence and experience.
Showjumping	jumping over coloured poles in an arena.
Spooky	a term used when a horse gets frightened easily.
Stock	a type of necktie worn when competing.
Sweet Itch	a condition horses get when they are allergic to little biting flies like midges. It makes their manes and tails very itchy and they have the urge to scratch on anything to hand.
Twitch	a piece of thin rope on a stick which twists round the upper lip and when moves gently sooths the horse and calms it.
Unaffiliated Events	usually local shows that anyone can enter.
Warmblood	a type of horse.
Windsucking	a term used when a horse sucks on the top of a door or fence post.
Withers	the part of a horse which sticks up at the bottom of their neck.
Wobblers Syndrome	a condition affecting the discs on the spine which makes the horse wobbly in appearance when it moves.

Working Hunter   a showy-type competition where you jump a course of natural fences in an arena and then your horse is judged on its movement.

Printed in Great Britain
by Amazon

A year can go by in a gallop when you're a horsey mum, so when William joined Linda Robins' already raucous mob to begin his training one July, she decided to start a diary of all the dramas down in the yard.

Often hilarious, sometimes tragic and always hectic, William, Ben, Teddy and Midi's frolics (not to mention those of a good few other characters) is a warm insight into the inner circle of a horsey family. With helpful hints and tips on training and owning horses, whether you're a novice or an old hand, *Diary of a Horsey Mum* is sure to begin an obsession all of your own.

Linda Robins is a married mother of two who has always been passionate about horses. She particularly loves training and re-training horses, treating them as part of the family, and competes in various disciplines whenever she has the chance.

ISBN 978-1-84748-569-4

UK £8.99 US $14.95

9 781847 485694

ATHENA PRESS

www.athenapress.com